walk specifi

and achievement

to put to pen these many God-sent revelations of HIS faithful inspiration in our lives.

George Hicker

President, Cardinal Industrial Real Estate

I find this inordinately well written work to be inspirational. It presents powerful, emotionally charged narratives about the inhumanity of racism in a sensitive manner. The writer is a person of good will that poignantly depicts how the human spirit, human nature, and human faith can overwhelm racism.

Augustus A. White, III, M.D., Ph.D.

Orthopaedic Surgeon-in-Chief Emeritus, Beth Israel Deaconess Medical Center
Former Master of the Oliver Wendell Holmes Society, Harvard Medical School
Ellen and Melvin Gordon Professor of Medical Education
Professor of Orthopaedic Surgery at the Harvard-MIT Division of Health Sciences and Technology

As I read the excerpt you sent, I was reminded of how great and important our families and the families of our friends are to our overall development. Your stories remind us of our stories and how God uses people in our lives.
Excellent read . . .

Jim Russell

Executive Pastor, Mariners Church

Willie Naulls is a man of character and his values and passion come across effortlessly in his writing. I've known Willie for years and have always admired his faith, strength, character and his relationship with God.

Billy Donovan

Head Men's Basketball Coach, University of Florida
Back-to-Back NCAA Champion as Coach

Great Things

GOD

Has Done

Willie Naulls

with Lisa Naulls

Library of Congress Cataloging-in-Publication Data

Naulls, Willie, and Naulls, Lisa
Great Things God Has Done

ISBN 978-0-9763709-4-9

1. Naulls, William D. (Willie)
2. Athletics – Philosophy
3. Religion
4. Conduct of Life

Cover design by Lisa Naulls
Interior design by Dr. Anne Van de Water Naulls

Photo on back cover by Pam Green
Photo at top of page 216 by Kori Withers

The names of some of the people in these true stories have been changed to protect their wishes for privacy.

Published by Willie Naulls Ministries
Post Office Box 132888
Spring, Texas 77393-2888
www.willienaulls.org • willie@willienaulls.org

Manufactured in the United States of America
International Standard Book Number: 978-0-9763709-4-9

Special Thanks

The publication of

Great Things God Has Done

is made possible by generous contributions from

George and Kathy Hicker

and

The A. A. White Family Fund

Dr. Anne Van de Water Naulls
my wife and partner
Without you, this important work together
with God would not have matured
I love you

Table of Contents

Introduction

Willie, you asked about what God has done in our lives. As you know, most of those responses are very personal. Of course, God is always there working for us even when we don't acknowledge it; but I've been aware of His presence a lot lately. I didn't answer, because my pains are still very fresh and I didn't want to start crying again.

I think you know that my brother committed suicide right before Christmas. I'm still having a very difficult time dealing with this loss; but I thought you might like to know what God did immediately to ease my suffering. Somehow He made sure that I was in the exact right place and at the exact right time with the exact right person when I got that news!

That day I had a strong urge to go to the bookstore at our church. They have a great selection of Christian literature, but they also have some neat tape sets (series, sermons, etc) and some delightful gift items. I was drawn to do some Christmas shopping there, and I had just selected my gift items and was checking out when the county coroner from Indiana called on my cell phone to tell me what had happened to my brother! The ladies working at the store could tell that something was horribly wrong, and they immediately called the church office. One of the pastors came down to get me and led me to the library where we sat and talked for over an hour. I know God was speaking through him. He was such a comfort, and he was able to help me plan what I needed to do and say to notify my family about what had happened. He made sure that I was in full control before I drove home. I felt that he was God's special messenger to me, as this particular pastor moved to another position in ministry at another church shortly after he helped me that day.

When I think back on all the thousands of places I might have been when I got that news and how dangerous it might have been had I been driving, it amazes me to realize how God orchestrates the details of our lives. We serve an awesome God, and often fail to recognize all the blessings He bestows!

Keep up your work in His service, and may His abundant blessings always be yours.

Thanks again, Diane

Our friend Diane's email shares a wonderful example of the innumerable ways in which God shows His love to people. This book of short stories is an outpouring of what great things God has done to change the way we think about Him and each other. Evidence of God's supernatural intervention into the lives of ordinary people like you and me encourages our faith to trust Him in any situation. Transparent testimonies can serve to both edify and heal. They demonstrate that God does not show favoritism.

Answered prayers are powerful to teach lessons that change our minds about who God is, and can be, to anyone who trusts Him. Tragedies, expressed through heartfelt experiences, are very personal. When shared in a non-threatening, storytelling manner, they have the power to draw people to the source of healing, Jesus Christ. Each story included herein challenges you, whatever your station in life, to pursue our loving God. The answered prayers of these blessed people will inspire you to want to know better our Creator, whose love transcends cultures and generations.

This book is dedicated to you. God wants you to trust Him. I am grateful to the many brothers and sisters who shared what great things God did in their lives. I thank God for the honor to write down His miraculous signs and wonders to behold. These glimpses into the lives of Christian men and women will change the way you think about God.

Willie Naulls

Did You Ever. . . . Did You?

I

Did you ever feel:
wired in fear
with nothing to hold dear
any moment a tear
your future unclear . . .
did you?

. . .

V

Did you ever joy when:
from the west Hope came
and He knew you by name
He and your Mom thought the same
inspiring you to get into life's game . . .
did you?

DIP-er-DUNK

The mid-morning sun peeked its rays through the clouds across our small backyard. Competition for space for relief from the effects of heavy rain of the previous days was evident. Chickens and our goat joined my brother Billy and me on the only dry ground near the back door of our side of a rented duplex. This was our designated play area when Mom and Dad were at work. We were taught that obedience to their words was critical for survival in the segregated environment into which we had been born.

"William, can you come out and play?"

Alphonso's loud voice was a welcome interruption. I leapt up, opened the screen door and vaulted through the three rooms of our small home. I was happy to see my best friend's smiling face when I opened the front door.

"You want to go down to the new public swimming pool? It just opened last week."

"My mom's not home so I can't. Don't know how to swim either."

"They'll teach us how."

"Let me ask my brother if he wants to come with us. He's almost eight now, you know." I walked uncertainly back through the house, looked through the screen door and inhaled to give momentum to my confidence. "Billy . . . do you . . . ."

"Nope," he shot back without looking up from repairing his cherished skate-mobile. "And you can't either. Mama told you not to even think about doing something she doesn't know about. You go with Alphonso and you'll get into big trouble."

I grumbled all the way back through the front

door and sat down on the wall that kept our yard from eroding into the street. "I can't go."

"Just walk with me down there. It's so far. I don't wanna go by myself. My daddy and mama aren't home either. We'll get back before they do. They'll never know."

I don't know what came over me. "Okay – let's go." I jumped to my feet in full stride. Didn't even look back to make sure the front door was closed.

We sprinted up the dry side of Church Street, then turned left across Alphonso's lawn at the corner of Fleming Avenue. At the next corner, I froze. "What do we do now? Mama told me to never cross Eighth Street without her."

"I cross here with my dad all the time to go to the store. We just have to be careful, that's all, and run fast when there's no traffic," Alphonso assured me.

Mom had told me no colored people could live or play on Eighth Street. Danger was on my mind. At the right moment, we crossed, then continued down Fleming and passed Miss Billie Montgomery's kindergarten, my first school. I had never been this far from home without Mom. We took caution to jump clear of mud puddles. I started to get a little scared. Strange people stared, strange dogs barked, big trees hung over the unpaved street. Weird sounds of insects echoed around my head. Our pace quickened.

We jogged, sometimes sprinted. At the moment that I sensed a nauseating, uncomfortable feeling in my stomach, the sound of kids playing stilled the slide. What seemed to be hundreds of kids having the time of their lives echoed throughout. We sprinted past the "Colored Only" sign into unscripted euphoria. I stood, mesmerized. The midday humidity and 98° heat scorched my sweat drenched body. Someone splashed water on

Alphonso. Before I could collect my thoughts, he was out of his shoes into the shallow end.

"Come on in, William. The water feels really good."

A big boy, about twelve years old – I think his name was Felton -- beckoned. "Come on in. Don't be scared. Give me your hand. I'll help you. Don't be scared."

Off with my shoes and socks, I joined them. The water level was between my knees and my chest. It felt really good all right. I exhaled to experience this new sensation as the cool water splashed all over my body.

"Take my hand and I'll help you learn to swim in the deep end," Felton offered. "That's how you learn to swim. I'll help you."

I remembered Alphonso said they would teach us. His grip grew firmer and more uncomfortable as we moved toward the serious end of the pool.

"Stop. Let me go. I don't want to go any deeper . . . ," I gurgled.

His face took on a sadistic twist in glee as he pulled me under. I resisted with all my strength, but he persisted, deeper. My demand for freedom lasted for what appeared to be an eternity. The blank expressions on the faces of bystanding kids frustrated hope. I inhaled; my lungs filled. As I came up for the second time, my thoughts frantically called Mama for help.

* * *

The warm concrete against the side of my face, a faint voice over the murmur of kids' chatter, graced my choking motions back to consciousness. "Can you hear me, William?" The voice knelt and spoke softly close to my ear. "Are you all right, baby?" It was Mama. How did she know? Guilt gripped my soul.

"Yes, Mama. I never should have come down here without asking first," I cried. "I'm sorry, Mama."

"Shh-h-h-h, baby. Hush now. God has given you back to me and that's all that matters. I ran all the way down here as soon as Billy told me where you and Alphonso had gone. The devil tried to kill you but he can't have you." She paused and took a deep breath. Looking up toward heaven, she said, "Thank you, Lord, for the angels you have assigned to protect my family." Her attention shifted back to me, "You feel well enough to get up, baby?"

"Yes, Mama. I feel better." I coughed some more chlorinated water out as she helped me to my feet.

"I'm sorry, Mrs. Naulls. I was just playing." Felton appeared remorseful as he glanced down at me. "I'm sorry, William. I'll never do nothing like that again."

Mama stared into his eyes. Her pointing finger pierced his chest. "You go on home, boy, and pray to God for forgiveness. We'll see you with your mama and daddy in church on Sunday." She turned and smiled toward a young woman. "God bless you, honey. You pulled my boy out of that water, and I thank you. May the Lord multiply His return to you and your family. He loves you, you know."

The girl nodded as tears mounted to a stream. "Yes, Ma'am, Mrs. Naulls. I'll see you in church too."

"Get your things and come on, William and Alphonso." She grabbed my right hand and his left and marched us toward home.

Word of my ordeal had reached Alphonso's mother before we arrived. When we neared her front door, he pleaded for a bond of silence about begging me to disobey Mom's orders.

Mrs. Randall rushed through the open door, hugged Alphonso to her ample bosom and stroked his head. "Are you all right, William?" Alphonso's unsmothered eye pleaded our code. "I'm so glad you're safe," his mother continued. "Praise the Lord."

"I'm fine, Mrs. Randall, thank you."

On the walk down the hill to our house in the middle of the block, Mama clutched me closer to her side. The dark clouds spread a gloomy cover across the skies as a bolt of lightning introduced the roar of thunder. "Be careful of those mud puddles."

She tightened the reins on my motion and stopped. We looked up to the sky, then around at the small houses lining both sides of the street as a light mist flushed our faces. "It sounds like more rain." She again scanned the houses along Church Street's muddy corridor. "God will provide a home with enough room for all of us – and on a paved street – one of these days." She waved to our neighbor as we neared home. "We've had a lot of rain but God sends it to cool His children in the heat of summer. I'm happy we live on the hill side of Church Street. The poor souls over there have flooded yards because of all the run-off from over here. Doesn't seem right, does it?"

"No, Mama."

Mom began to hum, then sing,

"Precious Lord, take my hand
Lead me on, help me stand
I am tired, I am weak, I am worn;
Through the storm, through the night,
Lead me on to the light:
Take my hand, Precious Lord,
Lead me home"

She paused, looked down at me. "I love you, William."

"I love you too, Mama. Will you sing that song

again? I love to hear you sing."

"Sure, honey, but don't forget – God loves you too. We have great plans, but you have to take better care of yourself when I'm not around. Do you hear me, William?" Her stern but soft voice was compelling.

My body quaked. The tears flowed unrestrained. "Yes, Mama. I will."

Mom never mentioned my unauthorized dip or the interrupted dunk again. She must have considered the near-death experience, an indelible imprint in my mind, punishment enough for my disobedience.

"Voices"

In the silence, of where I do hear
above the noises, where my thoughts are formed clear
come suggestions from two different voices
urgently appealing to counsel my choices

The decision is mine about which voice to trust
Even the unlearned knows information's a must
To make a choice that benefits my position
requires obeying the Voice that yields Godly fruition

Faith to choose a direction is a determination to walk
stepping out into the deep waters of which the voices talk
Now, there's this voice who cunningly imposes that wrong is right
But the One Voice who saved me says, Stand in the God kind of faith's fight

. . . .

Josie's Wail

Josie's slender frame is exaggerated by five feet ten inches of Texas bred and trained up swagger. She oozes confidence in whatever environment she finds herself. Experiences of growing up in the upper middle class community of Kingwood, Texas, trained her well and gave her the advantage that an informed young conservative Baptist is encouraged to live.

She met her husband, David, at Texas A & M University, where both attained graduate degrees, in nutrition and business administration respectively.

Their first child, Ricky, was born healthy and the expected "normal." This young couple was raised to expect nothing but the best from God. Life was exciting in the fast lane of socioeconomic upward mobility. When Josie confirmed the conception of their second child, David was equally elated. They both praised God and shared the good news with loved ones. The pregnancy was uneventful. The name Nicole was given prior to birth. Other than an early placenta previa, requiring two ultrasounds which further established little Nicole's development as normal, there was no reason to expect anything remotely related to what unfolded.

Nicole was born at Texas Women's Hospital after three hours of labor. During the first two post-partum days, Josie thought to go home, but her spirit didn't allow her to ask permission to leave the hospital. In hindsight, it was what she called "a God thing." Around two in the morning of her second day, Nicole stopped nursing and began a continuous weep which grieved Josie's soul. She knew this wasn't right and buzzed the nurse. "Will you please come in? Something is wrong with my baby." *Thank God we didn't go home,* raced through her mind.

As soon as could be arranged, Nicole was taken to the Neonatal Intensive Care Unit (NICU) to be diagnosed. Josie and David were informed by the neonatologist that the initial evaluation indicated a heart problem or meningitis, but the spinal tap was normal. They agreed to transfer Nicole to the NICU at Texas Children's Hospital. Empathically, the neonatologist asked in earnest appeal, "Keep me informed of Nicole's status. We love her."

Upon arrival, a Christian nurse prayed with David and Josie as yoked intercessors for Nicole. The pediatric cardiologist did an echocardiogram and pronounced the situation as grave. "There are a number of things wrong with Nicole's heart and pulmonary vessels between the heart and lungs. Your daughter probably won't survive. The problem with the pulmonary vessels is irreparable. I'm sorry to be the one to inform you, but . . . ." The doctor cleared his throat. "You should prepare yourselves to remove your baby from life support and let her go."

Josie and David stood momentarily transfixed as the weight of the bad report infiltrated. Then she said, "I need to be with my son. I can't touch or hold my baby daughter. I want to be with the living." Her eyes flooded. "Oh, God, heal my baby." A deep groan overflowed out of her heart.

They walked to the parking garage as one. David's lean, muscular form against hers encouraged their vows to unity through thick and thin. "God is right here with us. I sense His presence and His peace," David whispered as they began to appeal for mercy in prayer.

Josie's thoughts challenged God. She broke away from David, looked up and gestured with both arms toward heaven. "Why did you give me such confidence in You? My life has been story book. You've given me a great husband and a wonderful son. There were no complications. I trusted You – and now You take it out on my little helpless baby. You saw her lying there with all those tubes hooked up to keep her body functioning. Why her? Why not me?" She crumpled to the ground, hands over her face, screaming, "O, my Lord, please heal my baby!" In the midst of this crisis, she couldn't pray. Instead, she consciously turned her concerns over to the Holy Spirit to pray on her behalf."

David clutched Josie closer as he continued to acknowledge God's presence.

Josie called members of their Sunday school class to request the church family's prayers for God's intervention. Subsequently, a special time of prayer was called at their church and was attended by her parents.

In the early evening, hope spoke the good report of faith. "The pulmonary vessels are OK. The aorta is not attached correctly to the heart. Also, there are two holes in the heart. We are confident we can fix those problems. She is not completely out of the woods, but we're on our way."

God's team of praying parents, believers, friends, family members around the country, physicians, nurses and hospital personnel came together in obedience to His Word. He heard the earnest appeal of Josie and David. Nicole was stabilized in the hospital for a week. God's devout surgical nurse spoke His encouragement into David and Josie." Dr. Mac has agreed to do Nicole 's surgery. He's the best in the world."

The preliminary report was not the final reality. Staff doctors thought they might have to do a temporary procedure, with additional surgeries later on. They postulated that Nicole could be very sick for a year as what they called a "blue baby."

The God kind of faith rose up and shouted through Josie's trained up swagger of confidence, "NO! Not my daughter!"

Her eyes blazed in righteous indignation at the thought of a bad report of doubt about Nicole. After all, hadn't Jesus promised, "If you just believe, you will see the glory of God." As Lazarus was called forth from death, so little Nicole was called forth by the Lord through David and Josie's faith, to reveal the glory of God.

When all the tests showed overwhelming odds that Nicole would have serious ramifications from the problems with her heart valves, Josie screamed, "NO! Not my daughter!" Dr. Mac spoke the word of hope, optimistically declaring, "I have to actually look at Nicole 's heart during surgery to confirm or reject the suggested possibilities of the ultrasound."

The eleven-hour surgery was performed on Friday, 25 July 2003, beginning at eleven in the morning. Sixteen hours later, at three o'clock on Saturday morning, Dr. Mac reported, "She's fine. We just attached the aorta to the heart. No extensive repairs were required of her valves. They are smaller than normal because of the minimal blood that has flowed through them. We'll monitor them over time and they should grow. By the way, make sure everybody knows an important fact." He stopped in humble awe. Tears welled up as he pointed a finger upward. "I didn't heal the valves in Nicole's heart."

News of Nicole's response to God's nurturing through the many people He called to serve her inspired celebration to erupt in joyous praise to the Lord. As David sat looking at his beautiful infant daughter, he was reenergized to be her father in the Spirit of our Father God. With his face a few inches from hers, she acknowledged his presence by squeezing his little finger, "really hard."

Nicole was out of the hospital in two weeks. Six months later, the valves had grown to normal size. She has never required additional surgery and all of her frequent checkups have resulted in excellent reports.

Josie's thoughts reflect a truth for all to ponder. "Looking back, I am sometimes overcome with emotion and cry; yet I wouldn't change the experience. I have at times felt guilty for my thoughts of questioning God, but I have learned to have a more honest relationship with Him. I know that God knows my thoughts and emotions already. The difference is, I now feel free to intentionally share any and everything with Him. He is more real to me now."

David concluded, "We are just a normal couple and don't have super faith. We just turned everything over to God, and it was all Him."

Isn't this a good reminder for all of us?

Repentance

Camouflaged – where my soul does mourn
mixed in wail of past mental scorn
I long to forgive – and forget – what my heart does sentence
constantly awake in me is the thought – true repentance

. . . .

Every man and woman in ministry is faced with this dilemma
Only a humble walk in the faith of Christ counters this enigma
Examine who you think to be, and pray to find out who you ain't
The Lord rebukes each one of us who is an unrepentant saint

Forgetting is the Better Part of Forgiving

I labored young for my money
I played hard to earn me some fame
But through it all I realized
Forgiveness is life's hardest game

"Your daddy promised to never treat me disrespectfully again. He asked me to come home, to forgive him, and I did."

Mom taught me that love matures forgiveness. In her gentle committed persistence, after a year of separation from my brother Billy and me, she blended back into our daily lives without causing a wave. Her submissive disposition invaded a resolve of silence and mental isolation between my father and me. We all gradually communicated better as I responded in more than one word answers to her empathic questions about what was going on in my life.

"Lionel, an older kid who practices basketball with me at the rec center, works on the docks unloading cargo from international merchant ships. Mr. Duffy, his uncle, is a member of the Longshoremen's Union. They invited me to go with them to the Union Hall in Wilmington. Even though I'm only 12, they think I look old enough to get by the age screening. Mr. Duffy has seen me play sports and says I'm strong enough to do the work."

Mom gave me her blessing. "Take care of yourself. Don't try to do anything beyond your capacity. You're still a very young man, William. Be careful working with all those grown men!" I liked it that she called me a young man rather than a boy.

The first day went like clockwork. Lionel and his uncle picked me up at the bottom of the project's hill at six-thirty. Mr. Duffy's old Chevy truck sputtered all the way to the Union Hall. "Get a 'pea,' a number from that box on the front counter. That places you in numerical order to be called for work, after the Union members have all been sent out on jobs," Lionel whispered up to my ear behind the shield of his hand. He stood about six inches shorter than Mr. Duffy's six-foot frame. At six-foot-four, I was taller than most of the men so I decided to sit in a corner in an attempt to be less conspicuous.

"TWENTY-FIVE!" The voice startled me. I leapt up and hurried to the window. The gentleman took my #25 "pea" and never asked my age.

"Fill this paper out and bring it right back." I did and, without a word, he gave me a slip with information about where I was to report. I walked out the door without a clue about how to get there.

"Do you need a ride? I think we're going to the same job," a total stranger asked.

"Thank you, sir!" I hopped in the back of his pickup truck. Lionel waved as he left toward a different work location. I was on my own.

At the job site a man with a clipboard stood on a platform with a group of men assembled around him and passed out work assignments. After all of the men left in response to his pointing, he looked in my direction. My heartbeat accelerated as his hand extended to receive my slip; then he gave me a directional nod.

"Thank you, sir." I sprinted over to the work station where I would spend the next eight hours and many more during the weeks that followed.

Standing beside a cargo ship gave me a completely different perspective. I had watched many come and go through the San Pedro Harbor.

My vantage point had always been from atop the hill on which my family lived in the housing project, Western Terrace. That day I would discover first hand what was inside those large ships, at least this one which I and others were being paid to unload. It was bananas – by the stalk – and with the biggest tarantulas imaginable.

My eyes scanned upward to glimpse the first stalks to emerge. The ship's deck stood about ten stories above the dock. Out of its belly came my responsibility and test of developing manhood. A few moments later, those first stalks descended on individual compartments resembling seats on a Ferris wheel. They were then taken off and placed on several belts running perpendicular to the ship. I stood mesmerized at the end of our conveyor belt which began at the ship and ran between two rows of box cars, fifteen on either side. Each man had his own car to fill. My muscles flexed; my mind soared. "I'm ready. Bring it on. I can do this," exploded out in a controlled self-assuring grunt. What my partner on the opposite side of the belt and I were supposed to accomplish became apparent: Take every banana stalk reaching our location off the belt and place them carefully upright inside the box cars.

"Hopefully those fourteen guys on each side of the belt up the line will do their share of the work. Whatever they don't get becomes our job," Melvin informed me. He chuckled, smiled, and shrugged his shoulders. "If we don't pull everything that comes this far, they'll fall off the end of the belt down there on the railroad tracks. The boss don't like that, young blood." His blond hair stuck out from under the baseball cap hiding his forehead as he grinned from ear to ear flashing sparkling teeth and gums.

"Oh, is that why nobody wants location number fifteen?" I smirked. Attempts at humor were new.

The first hour was a breeze. "Two guys up the line took a bathroom break and two more went to get water. Get ready for the avalanche, young blood." I got my first understanding of why no one wanted the last station. We unloaded seventy- to ninety-pound stalks of bananas as fast as we could, frantically piling them on the ramp before they ended up on the tracks. In desperation, I pressed the emergency stop button. We looked up the line for empathy. The red lights overhead flashed and the sirens blared, featuring us as the two guys who couldn't keep up with the flow.

The supervisor's loud Southern voice roared, "Come on, young blood, you gotta keep up!"

Workers on either side of the belt unloaded the brunt of their jokes and laughter on us. "Come on, young blood. You're holding us up. The bananas and spiders are waiting!"

I rushed the overflow of stalks into the box car, apologized to the foreman and pushed the button to resume the flow of "nannas." A roar and sarcastic applause erupted at the sound of the belt's movement.

By the end of the day I was exhausted and hungry. I'd forgotten my lunch, had no money to buy food and refused handouts from concerned men at my side. The spent state from hard work felt real good in my mind and body as I walked the five miles home.

When I reached the top of the hill, there my Mom stood, smiling. "Aren't you hungry? You forgot your lunch."

My heart leapt inside. "Yes, Mama, I did and I'm real hungry."

She drew nearer, tugged my shirt. "How was your first day on the docks?" My muscles twitched from exhaustion as we went up the sidewalk and ascended the five stairs into our home. "Wash up. I have a surprise for you." Minutes later she placed before me a plate filled with spaghetti and meat sauce. "You did a man's day of work and you need a man's portion of food." She sat down on the other side of the table. After we prayed, she reiterated, "What was it like today?"

"I learned that it is very important to do my share. It was hard work but I feel really good about myself. I can do it, Mama."

"I know you can, honey. I never doubted that." Mom looked pleased to watch me vacuum down the spaghetti and garlic toast. She asked, "What type of men did you meet? What impressions did you form?"

No other family members seemed to care except Jerry, my younger brother, who sat on the wooden floor next to her chair. "Can I come to work with you tomorrow?" he asked.

"Not just yet. I'm barely old enough and you're only nine. How was your day at work, Mom?"

A sparkle radiated in her eyes as her face flushed to reddish brown. "Oh, the time passes real fast when you're busy and have things to do. Thank you for asking, William." She lowered her head. I was confused by the watering in her eyes. She looked up slowly. "Thank you for caring enough to ask." A momentary focus on her passed quicker than it came.

After a long shower, I began organizing for the next day. On the night stand was my baseball glove, a reminder that our team had a championship game in a few days.

"Mom, please wake me up early so I have time to walk to the Union Hall. I definitely want to be on time to get my 'pea.'"

"I'll get you up in plenty of time." Her soft lips on my forehead settled my thoughts into sweet slumber.

The next morning my feet hit the floor as soon as Mom's gentle voice awakened me. I washed up, dressed, ate a large bowl of oatmeal and three pieces of cinnamon toast, and was out the door in twenty minutes. "I'm gonna pull me some bananas off that belt today" was my departing declaration.

On the main highway, a truck stopped and waited. I recognized the head out the window. It was Melvin. "You want a ride, young blood?"

I jumped on the back of the truck and smiled. "Thanks!" The morning wind swirled around my head as my thoughts reflected the movement. It is really good to be alive here in California. I had comfort in knowing that the White men driving up front were not planning to make me a victim of a lynch mob. When we left the South four years earlier, my father and mother prayed to God that California would be the environment where their children could grow up and not be hated because of the color of our skin.

As we neared our destination, I noticed the fast pace of people in the streets, on their way to work, away from this run down industrial section of town. I thanked Melvin and his father as we walked together from their truck into the little store front Union Hall already jammed with men.

I didn't get work consistently but was excited when I got the checks for the times I did a longshoreman's day. To earn money built up my sense of self worth. Weekly lawn cutting customers told me they were very satisfied, so time was filled with productive enterprise that increased my self confidence and sense of growth toward independence.

Our baseball coach appeared happy to see me at the park practicing on the days I didn't get work. "Naulls, the big game is a few days away and you haven't been consistently at practice. Will you be ready?"

"Yes, sir, coach! I am ready. Thank you for excusing me from practice. The extra money I earn helps my family."

"I hope my boys learn that same attitude. You're a good son."

"Thank you, sir."

* * *

It doesn't seem so long ago that I was twelve years and living in a low-income housing project in San Pedro. As a developing young athlete, my daily life consisted of home chores, school, work, sports and eating enough food. Our housing project baseball team was without uniforms and had limited equipment. In spite of that, we advanced to the Southern California Junior Championship game. It was scheduled to be played in Torrance, an upwardly mobile middle class all-White community.

It is difficult to describe in words how excited I was. To my well fed fantasy, this championship game was like the World Series. Our family had no TV, but every day during baseball season I listened to recreated professional games on the radio. The announcer, Hal Berger, put us listeners in front row seats. The Dodgers of Brooklyn, New York Yankees, Boston Red Sox, Saint Louis Cardinals, Detroit Tigers, Cincinnati Reds were right there in my bedroom. Every pitch of Bob Feller's 100 mph fast ball or Mel Parnell's curve ball was delivered to me at bat. My mind exploded with possibilities as this announcer took listeners on mental trips describing cities and ball parks that I thought were in another world, on another planet. I read books and did reports for school assignments on the legends of baseball, such as Christy Mathewson and Cy Young. There were no major league professional sports teams in southern California. Over the years the stories of legendary baseball players' lives and African-American players – like Jackie Robinson, Larry Doby, Roy Campanella and Don Newcombe – and their breakthrough of racial barriers became hope to get away from what I perceived to be my dad's evil rule. These athletic heroes inspired me to do something with my life. Driven and motivated, I dreamed of the day I would be at bat, and on the pitcher's mound, in professional baseball.

The young men on our project's team represented a wide cross-section of the minority racial groups from around the world. Families sped to the port of San Pedro from the Philippines, Yugoslavia, Italy, South and Central America, Mexico, and as far away as China. Most of the parents of the starters on our team had migrated from the South, as my family had. We were consciously united in the new sense of freedom we experienced in San Pedro. Daily we had open communication with people of all skin colors for the first time in our lives.

It was with this new conscious comfort in integrated situations that we embraced the magnitude of this inter-community baseball game. For the first time, it pitted the district's undefeated winners of the *have-nots* against the perennially undefeated winners of the *haves*. The walk from San Pedro to the game site was several miles. Most, if not all, of our parents were at work. Our opponent was a well-oiled, well-trained, disciplined baseball organization. They had as much financial support, coaching, equipment, uniforms, and community support as any team has ever had or needed in the history of youth amateur sports. The biggest problem they faced was holding back laughter as we arrived one by one, sometimes two or three together, without the appropriate baseball attire. Our opponents laughed and pointed at us like we were a circus coming to town.

"You ready, Naulls?" Coach Bob Wyrick studied me for a response.

"Yes, sir. I'm ready." I stared back at him expressionless. He looked like the actor Van Johnson.

"How did you get here?"

"I walked. Here come some of the guys now. We are ready!"

"Can you talk your brother into catching? Joe said you threw too hard last game and his thumb is still swollen."

"I'll ask him when he gets here. Billy is older so I can't talk him into doing anything."

What I remember vividly from that pre-game scene was the look of over-confidence in the actions of our opponents. Their superiority complexes spilled over into condescending laughter and finger-pointing remarks which demonstrated their disdain toward us *have-nots*.

I stood on the pitcher's mound, staring at my brother for a sign, poised to make the first pitch of the game. As all in attendance inhaled to begin this historic encounter, the opposition's coach's voice burst through the suspended silence. "Hey you, Willie or whatever they call you. You're nothing but a big ugly NIGGER! You look like a clown out there, all of you. No uniforms. You are a disgrace to baseball and you should be in a zoo with the rest of the animals."

Momentarily paralyzed by this bold, unexpected verbal attack, I shifted my eyes across the space between us. His young players – and their parents – all laughed, and some even echoed this man's hostility. Even the umpire was amused as he smirked and shouted, "Play ball!"

I filled my eyes to record in my mind the image of this group of fellow humans, then tuned out their hostile words. What I saw was fear and insecurity in their eyes. My mother said that fear and insecurity were man's basis for hating Black men. Rage, inspired by their words, reared up in my soul. Retribution was as fire burning in my bones. I suppressed tears as I recorded every face bobbing up and down like Ping-Pong balls afloat on rapids behind their dugout's fencing. Their words to incite instability imploded in them as the game progressed. I had been raised to not give in to verbal attacks. Even today that framed image of the fear on their faces passes before me to forgive and forget. In response to their hostility, I had a conditioned reflex. "Move from the distracting frame to the next. My purpose: to get out the first batter standing at the plate," I spoke out loud, to remind myself.

As I walked toward our dugout at the end of the fifth inning, I peeked a glance under the bib of my cap at that same group. Their self-debasing tactics had attempted to move our team away from the task at hand. "We came here to win this game," I shouted to remind my teammates as we sat down in the dugout. Our competition now appeared dazed in disbelief. Not only had I struck out fourteen of the fifteen batters they sent up to the plate, but I had dominated them with my own bat. Two home runs and a double. Eight RBIs. To reverse my drift toward a prideful mindset, words of caution reminded me of two things. I stood and repeated them: "Don't mirror evil but be gracious in victory and defeat! Never count the chickens before they hatch."

The last batter swung and missed my final 90+ mph fast ball. He was the nineteenth batter of the twenty-one I faced who turned away in disgust toward his dugout. Not one of their players reached first base. The only two batters to hit the ball in fair territory grounded out from third to first. This was the first perfect no hit /no run game of my pitching career. Final score: 17 to 0. My teammates mobbed me on the pitcher's mound. The other team came forth in awe of our force. They apologized for their vulgar remarks. The coach, through his wrinkled, cigarette-stained lips, said, "Willie, I was only trying to get you off your game so we could win." Without a word or facial reaction, I nodded and pivoted away with a tug on my cap. This scene was recorded as an indelible mental scar. I towered physically over that group of “new fans” who had, with seared conscience, viciously inflicted on my soul a weight that brings tears to my eyes as I write about it today. That mean spirit haunted my trust in people for years.

Does this emotion prove I haven’t forgotten? Have I forgiven? Yes, I sincerely believe that I have forgiven. But does not the fact that I still remember violate God’s standard of forgiving? I saw that coach and some of his players over my high school and college years. We never made eye contact, but I heard their whispers whenever we met on any playing field. Our San Pedro teams never lost to their teams in any sport. One of those opposing players was my college basketball teammate at UCLA and became a medical doctor. We never discussed "the game" because he never brought it up. But I could see self-condemnation in his eyes.

I have often wondered what happened to all those players, on both teams. How were the "givers" and "receivers" affected mentally by that evil spirit who used the opposing coach to lead his players down a perverted path? His words promoted a separatist agenda for youth baseball. As future competitors in the open market, how were they affected by "the game"? Did my teammates forgive and forget? Did the opposition forgive themselves? Did they learn anything from their weak tactics? Were their seeds dried up and unproductive on the earth because they didn't seek forgiveness from God? I never prayed that God would forgive them until now. But – I forgave them.

Today, I have prayed to God and thanked Him that He will forgive all who ask. To forgive is to forget, never to hold the wrong done you against that person or persons again. Godly forgiveness is our standard. He never remembers our sins forgiven. God says Forgiving is Forgetting, never to remember again.

Did You Ever Wish?

Did you ever wish you had a dad
the thought of whom didn't make you sad?
His memories causing your insides to smile
giving you peace, being there all the while?

Idealistic I know to think this way
'cause "truth's in the puddin'" as do "they say"

But what a relief, if in his tracks to trek
in anxious moments when satan's agents beck
If dad could have been there as a light to guide
through tough decisions, our hands held at his side
. . . .

What do I say to young folk, as God's teacher on call?
Whom to recommend as model for hearts to install?

Thank God for His answer, with no shadow to shift
Anchor your heart in Jesus, and don't let Him drift

The Hound of Heaven Perseveres

"The Youngest Evangelizes the Eldest"

Jimmie focused on each student's personal summation of the benefit received from the twelve-week course, "An Assembly on Cultural Sensitivity." Robin said, "Believing that I receive what I pray for when I pray – before the physical manifestation – continues to be my greatest challenge, Pastor Willie."

There was an "uh-huh" nodding of heads in agreement hum. This was the core group of seekers of the Truth. The class membership had reached 31 at its peak registration.

"Members of my Sunday school class have prayed for two years for my older brother's salvation, and nothing has happened." Jimmie's eyes moistened. "My brother continues to hurt so many members of our family. He's the head of his family, the strong influence over his children and grandchildren." He bowed his head, put his hands over his face and wept.

"Our job is to talk to non-believing relatives and pray for their salvation," Frank offered. "That's all you can do, Jimmie. God has His own timing. Trust in Him. Have His kind of faith. Be patient. God is faithful and trustworthy."

An impeccably dressed and groomed gentleman, Jimmie has been married to his beautiful, Spirit-filled wife, Elsa, for 34 years. They are faithful members of their church, where they are loved and highly respected. He followed a friend down the aisle at a tent revival meeting and joined the church at the age of nine, but consciously committed his life to the Lord in 2000.

Born in the small segregated farming community

of Alma in northwest Arkansas, he, his sister and two brothers were bussed 13 miles to the school for Blacks in Fort Smith. An outstanding student athlete, he achieved All-State honors as a cornerback in football before joining the Marine Corps at 19 in 1966. He was shipped to Viet Nam the next year.

His parents were honest, hard working Christians. They raised their four children on a farm in a small, four-room bungalow, with an outhouse. His mother was the committed homemaker, choir director and spiritual helpmate of her husband. Discipline was his father's successful task. He oversaw shotgun weddings for both of Jimmie's brothers, standing behind his word: "If you sleep with a young lady and get her pregnant, you better make sure she's the one you wanna marry, 'cause as long as you're under my roof and I'm alive, you will marry her. I'll see to that!"

Since his rededication to the Lord, Jimmie has spent the last eight years evangelizing. He serves his church and community with commitment to excellence in the Lord. Whether police chief or elder or choir member, everyone soon observed that he was a man faithful to God's Word. Yet he had a burden in his heart. "My own family members – especially my eldest brother James – are hopelessly lost, going to hell. I have prayed to God, over and over, by myself and with others, for my family. For years I asked God to tenderize their hearts. I've prayed and prayed and prayed. I'm tired. The Lord is using me here in Texas, while my entire family is lost. I'm so discouraged."

"Consider what God is about to say, Jimmie." He directed his attention to hear what Pastor Willie had to say. "When you pray a petition to the Lord according to His Word, He hears you. And if you have conviction, that He hears you, your prayer is answered. You don't have to pray that prayer of petition over and over again because God has already heard your prayer and set the answer in motion. Thereafter you should pray a prayer of thanksgiving. This would demonstrate that you believe that God heard and answered your prayer when you prayed. Jesus told us to have the God kind of faith. Believe that you receive God's answer to your prayer when you pray, and you will see the glory of God. That's the God kind of faith the Holy Spirit has taught us in this class for the last several weeks."

Jimmie's eyes widened. No man had been any more transparent than he was at that moment. "I'm tired. I prayed for James – we call him JC. He should be leading our family toward holy living. Instead, he acts like the devil himself, hurting his wife, their children and grandchildren, and everyone he can. He's bad news and I've given him up to hell. I've turned him over to satan because he's hopeless."

"Jimmie, you listen to me!" Jeanette stood up on the balls of her feet to maximize her 5′2″ impact. Her brown eyes flashed like caution lights warning of impending danger. "Don't you dare confess with your mouth that you've given up on your brother. You're the youngest child, but you're the one God has called. In you is the hope of salvation of your family. Jesus Christ in you is their only hope. You can't give up. You take the Word of God to your family. Could be you're the only one they'll listen to. Did you ever think of that?" She moved closer, to champion an in-your-face demand.

Jimmie looked shocked and convicted. Other students rushed to join Jeanette, laying hands on him to receive the chastisement of love from our heavenly Father through his obedient daughter, Jeanette. "Father God," she prayed, "use Jimmie in a mighty way to win his brother and family, who are lost in the darkness of sin, to you, Father. Change JC's role from being an agent of satan. Shake him up, Father, to know that he, the eldest son, is loved by the youngest enough to plead for his soul. Give my brother Jimmie the strength of conviction to not give up on JC because you haven't given up on him. We pray this in the mighty name of Your dear Son, Jesus Christ. Amen."

He wiped his eyes. "Thank you, Jeanette, for leading the class in intercessory prayer for me and my family. I will never forget it. Thank you, Pastor Willie, for teaching us to believe that we have what we pray for when we pray. Faith is . . . ."

"All praise be to God! Now go and pray for guidance about how to evangelize your own family."

What the class didn't know, Jimmie had recently been to Alma. There had been squabbling in the family over the occupancy of the home the heirs had been born in. It had been left to them by their parents with the stipulation that any of their children could live there if they paid the taxes. Jimmie and his middle brother, Cecil, agreed that JC's son Michael could live in the home. His kidneys had failed and he was on dialysis twice a week. JC was angry with Michael and attempted to have him evicted. He called the police to report drugs on the property which never materialized during their inspection. Jimmie finally realized the time had come for him to take action.

From his hotel room, he arranged a breakfast meeting with JC and Cecil. After he prayed, he shared with them his concern about their salvation. "You are doomed to go to hell, and you're leading your family there also." They glanced up under furrowed brows with heads still bowed. There was an audible groan from Cecil's spirit. Jimmie knew that God's Words convicted. Encouraged, he continued, "The prophet Hosea tells us 'people are destroyed from lack of knowledge. Because you have rejected knowledge, I also reject you . . . . I also will ignore your children.'

"Did you hear that clearly, brothers? I love you both and warn you that you have led your families away from the God of our childhood. Because you have rejected knowledge of God, He has rejected you. Hear what I am saying." Jimmie's voice escalated. "We were raised under the cover of our parents, who knew that 'the Lord is slow to anger, abounding in love and forgiving of sin and rebellion. Yet He does not leave the guilty unpunished.'" He stood over them with pointed finger and continued to quote Scripture. "'He punishes the children for the sin of the fathers to the third and fourth generation.'"

There was an eerie silence. Jimmie's eyes pleaded tears to be understood. The family situation was grave, hopeless. Only God's intervention could move the hearts of his brothers.

Cecil broke down. "I'm in agreement with what you want to do with the family." JC also nodded in agreement, but his grunting words sounded of head, not heart.

The three brothers agreed to convene a meeting at church the next day with the men of the family. The mission was to establish a Word-of-God-based standard by which the children and families would learn to live.

Back in his hotel room, Jimmie thanked God for beginning a work in his family, that he had believed deep in his heart was impossible. Why impossible? Because JC had embraced bitterness so deeply in his heart. He blamed his father for his unhappy marriage, in spite of the six children his first wife had borne him. He still mourned the death of eight year old Terry, his "favorite son." He diligently tried to drown his pain in alcohol. A second unhappy marriage and adulterous relationships had brought more children. JC's reputation was that of the lyrical rolling stone and his children followed the example. His mistrust of Michael was just the most recent indication of seething anger. Jimmie called him the "angry sinner" whereas Cecil, a lackadaisical but smiling alcoholic was the "happy sinner."

Three hours after meeting with his brothers, JC called. "I've changed my mind. The stuff I agreed to earlier, I've changed my mind." He hung up. Jimmie was crushed. He fulfilled his commitment to attend church services on Sunday, but left Alma on Monday.

He called JC two days later, only to find him still not in agreement. He kept praying, but was unsure and his intensity waned. He was thoroughly discouraged by his brother's stubborn rejection of the Lord's persistence and outstretched hands.

Jimmie's Sunday school class kept the faith of their united prayer for the family. But that night in the "Assembly on Cultural Sensitivity," Jeanette's stand on God's Word, by the Power of the Holy Spirit, encouraged Jimmie's faith to patiently persevere. "Loose your grip, satan, on JC's mind, in the Name of Jesus." The class members were on one accord.

Jimmie started praying the prayer of thanksgiving fervently and called JC Sunday night. No change in his attitude.

At six o'clock on Wednesday morning, the telephone startled his quiet prayer meditation. "Hello?"

"It's me, JC." He wept like a baby crying for milk. "Forgive me, Jimmie. I love you and thank you for not giving up on me. I won't fight against God any more. I'm going to ask all my children to forgive me, and all the other folk I've lied to and hurt. Do you think God will forgive me so my children and grandchildren won't go to hell? I don't want bitterness in my heart any longer."

"Don't ever doubt God, JC. He loves you and not only forgives those who ask for it out of a pure heart. He never remembers that sin forgiven."

Jimmie called him back that evening and two or three times a day all week, reassuring JC of his love and God's love.

On Saturday at five in the afternoon, Jimmie led JC in the sinner's prayer of salvation. JC accepted, becoming a newborn creation in Christ.

The following Saturday, JC called, excitement overflowing. "Jimmie," he gasped, "while I was working in my garden, I saw beautiful, ripe, juicy strawberries on one end of a row but smaller, under-producing plants at the other end. As I began to dig up the blighted strawberries, a Voice said to me, "I have not done this to you."

When JC called angry the next week, Jimmie counseled him. "Becoming a mature Christian doesn't happen overnight. You need to go to church and study God's Word." That Sunday, JC's voice on a phone message shared that he had met with Michael and was on his way out the door to attend church with his son.

Jimmie shared with faithful prayer partners of his church, "The new JC is being transformed by renewing his mind on the Word of God. He's excited about offering salvation to all in his voice's reach."

My Boyhood Dilemma

When I was just a little boy
I asked my mother, What will I be?
Will I be safe?
Will I be free?
How often did she say to me

You're no different from any other lad
It's what you choose to be, so be glad
Let the sky be your horizon
unlimited choices for you to work out
Be careful of sap sucking baggage
that impedes your daily best clout

. . . .

Lost 'n' Found

With no warning, Mom declared, "I'm finished with your father's abuse. He doesn't want me any more."

Her words shook the foundation of my stability. I trained up for life's possibilities under her exclusive voice. The self control she taught as a building block of character was tested at its mortar.

Mom's shoulders rounded as she lowered her head, in need of comforting arms. My eleven-year-old compassion hadn't matured to an appropriate response. I didn't know to give her back what she had always given me – unselfish, on-call love.

The jail time Dad had endured for physical abuse of Mom inspired self-encagement of his pent up rage. The resulting verbal assault Mom "refused to tolerate any more" was demeaning and mean spirited.

"I am confident that you and Billy can take care of yourselves."

Words, even today, inadequately describe the torment and pain that invaded as I watched Mom and my twin brother and sister board the Red Car for Los Angeles' Union Station. Beyond the train, large ships docked at Todd Shipyard, my father's employer. As far as the eye could see from the housing project's perch atop a hill in San Pedro, California, the mighty Pacific Ocean stretched through the harbor and out to vastness which appeared to run off the end of the earth. The train crawled forward. I couldn't tell if Mom saw me from inside, so I restrained the emotion to wave a scream. In silence, my older brother stood at my side the entire time, expressionless.

* * *

Mom, Jerry and Judy were expected back from Dallas at any moment. A year had passed since their departure. An uneasy anticipation clouded my mind. I kept the letters she had written in a box under my bed and reread them many times. Her abrupt departure and absence had taken their toll on my confidence to depend on her emotionally again.

Bonded in my soul, her first letter read, "I have confidence in you, William. I pray to God that you grow up to be a fine husband and father. Give your wife love and respect. Love each of your children as I have loved you. Please forgive me for leaving. I saw in your eyes the hurt you felt. I pray every day we'll all be together again. Take care of your father and brother. The Lord forgave us so that we can forgive them. You're strong. God's strength is magnified through us in forgiveness."

I put the letter back in the box, went back into the main room and sat down. The few dormant tears, that hurt had shed, dried up to protect the hardened state of my arid convictions. They were moistened in the thought of Mom's return and began to flow to wash away the ruptured lumps, melting the pain. It was gripping to hate my father and brother so intensely, yet it gave me a point to rally around to survive. I blamed them for abusing Mom to the point that she had no other choice but to leave to maintain her dignity. That letter whispered to my conscience, *To regain inner strength, I have to forgive.*

I looked around our home. We always referred to it as the large match box on stilts. The ungraded sloping topography required wooden four-by-four vertical beams to secure and level a foundation upon which to stabilize the small three-room project houses called Western Terrace. There were varying heights of crawl space underneath. Kids were advised to avoid these areas because of snakes and perceived instability of the structures in the event of an earthquake.

Home alone, I went from room to room checking for order. The largest room, with the entrance door in the center of the front wall, served as kitchen, dining room and living room. The couch on the opposite wall was my sister's bed at night. The one bathroom was on the entrance wall, separated from the kitchen by a common partition that jutted out toward the middle of the room. For the first time in our lives, we enjoyed an indoor hot-and-cold-water bathroom with a small shower. A kerosene stove stood in an adjacent space between the two areas. Dad's bedroom was to the right from the entrance door. My brother and I shared a room on the opposite end of the "match box." How could three more people fit in here? I pondered.

A faint sound of steps. I leapt up on the balls of my feet like a cat hearing a suspicious movement. From the screen door I could see her, a bag in each hand. She appeared to be dressed for summer and winter. The head scarf tied under her chin covered most of her face. Two young, serious faces at Mom's side beamed when they saw me. I stepped out, jumped off the tiered wooden steps to the ground.

She screamed, "William!" just as I yelled, "Mama!"

Our embrace bridged the gulf that separation had dug.

"My, how you've grown. You look so handsome and mature."

"I'm happy you came home, Mama." I squatted and hugged my eight year old siblings. "You two Texans all right?"

"The train ride was three days and three nights.

We're tired." Judy whined a smile as she rubbed her eyes.

Our neighbor, blonde hair curled up in rollers, stuck her head out the door and shouted, "Welcome home, Mrs. Naulls. We missed you."

"Thank you, honey."

I gestured toward the front door. "Let's go inside and you two can rest." We ascended the five steps into the house. "Where do I put the bags, Mama?"

With a pensive expression, she hesitated, right hand raised, pressed against her cheek. "Put my bag in your father's room. Your sister's bed is still the couch right here. Jerry will be moving back into you boys' room."

In a short time my father arrived with his favorite, my older brother. He appeared relieved to see Mom, and the twins were all over him and Billy.

In retrospect, order and the spirit of family returned with Mom. I thought she had been lured back by Dad's grip on her soul but soon realized that most important to her was to serve the quality of each of our lives. Her humble, steadfast commitment to do things God's way undergirded our individual growth. Our family was lost in disarray but found together again in answer to Mom's prayers.

Black Folks & White Folks

© 2003 William D. Naulls

Black Folks and White Folks, like Rhythm and Blues,
historically wed partners now paying some dues

Blacks brought here to feed, Whites bought into
the greed
but both came together wrought of satanic seed

. . . .

Knowing how tangled the web was spun,
how hatred of skin color was wickedly begun
try glorifying God in this lifetime to see,
people loving one another in Christ Jesus' decree

Alley-OOPS

I peered outside through a tear in the screen door. There were no signs of activity in the alley beyond our weather-beaten six-foot fence. My eyes shifted to the left edge of the back porch. Three pair of wet shoes sat drying just outside the laundry room door.

Saturday mornings were busy times in our home. Mom let us choose to help her before we could play. After cleaning the house inside and out, we helped wash the laundry for our family of six. Mom, on her washboard, scrubbed the clothes in the first tub, then put them in a tub of clear water for rinsing. My older brother Billy's job was to rinse each garment and run it through the hand wringer attached to the rinsing tub. The antiseptic aroma of Oxydol, Purex and P&G soap hovered around this exchange. My job was to catch and sort the garments and place them on a portable table. Mom then hung them on the clothes lines in the small side yard.

Our chore opportunity ended when all the starch pans, tubs, counters, tables, porch and floors were thoroughly clean. Later in the day, after playtime, the Naulls children were given the opportunity to iron our own clothes and shine our shoes for church and school.

My train of thought was broken as chickens began to scramble in a frenzy. Mr. Gibson, our landlord, scattered crumbs across the baked red clay between patches of grass. Mid-morning sunrays swirled steam off his bald head.

"How you doing this morning, William?"

"I'm fine, thank you."

"You be a good boy now and do what your mama tells you, you hear?"

"Yes, Sir, I will."

Large sunflowers peeked over the property boundary fence as he walked back through the door into his side of the little duplex our families shared.

"William?"

"Yes, Mama."

"What's so interesting out there in the yard?"

I backed away from the door, clearing my throat. "Nothing, Mama."

She spoke louder. "I feel sorry for that poor child. He's always hanging that small American flag through our gate to let you know he's available to play. He seems very lonely. But I've told you over and over again not to play with him. He lives across the alley and his daddy doesn't want him to be around you. I've told you not to go where you're not invited, haven't I?"

"Yes, Mama." *How did she find out about our secret signal,* I wondered. I eased over and peeked into the kitchen where she was baking a cake. She had invited our pastor to dinner on Sunday. "I noticed that the door to the toilet is open. Do you want me to close it?"

"Yes, thank you," she smiled.

The screen door barely cleared the outhouse and laundry room which had been added on to the house by Mr. Gibson, a plumber. I reached my left arm out and closed the door. As I turned to go back inside, my eyes sensed movement through a gap in the vertical boards of our rear gate. Jimmy Lee was just tall enough for me to see one eye, the freckles on his pale forehead and a few strands of strawberry blond hair standing straight up on the crown of his head.

"May I go up to Alphonso's house to shoot some marbles and say goodbye?"

After a pause she sighed my way, "All right, William, but if his parents aren't home I want you to come straight back here. You hear me?"

"Yes, Mama, I'll be back."

I sprang off the one step back porch and sprinted past the chicken coop that Mr. Gibson kept in the opposite corner of the yard. The chickens scattered and our old goat let out a baa-a-a-a. I reached up and pushed the two-by-four wooden latch which locked us in and danger out. Jimmy Lee beamed up at me as I stepped into the alley. He was a year older than I but a head shorter. We spoke in a whisper as we walked up the alley along the tire ruts in the red clay. The overgrowth between us was knee high the entire block between Jefferson Street and Fleming Avenue.

"My dad got a job in California. Mom said we're leaving town next week."

Jimmy Lee's expression changed. The peace we had as kindred spirits flipped to panicked desperation as of one falling backward off a steep cliff.

Tears streamed. "Why do you have to go away? You're the best friend I ever had," he gasped.

His emotional reaction summoned a tear to come forth from my left eye. I thought, *He is the only friend who is as quiet and introspective as I am. Neither of us likes noise or violence or aggressive intrusion.*

"Jimmy Lee?" His mother's voice startled us. It reverberated loud and clear off the walls along the alley and interrupted our bonding. "What have I told you about hanging around that boy and those people? Your dad is going to kill you and that boy too if he ever finds you together again." Her voice escalated as she pushed him almost to the ground. "Now get on your way home." She paused, turned and took three steps toward me. The hatred in her eyes, the twisted expression on her face, overwhelmed me with fear. I pivoted to run toward home. "Don't you ever come near my boy again, you dirty, stinking, nigger."

After a few strides, my mother's strong arms stopped me in a caress of comfort against her slight frame. She held me at arm's length and looked with concern into my eyes. "You all right, William? I heard the shouting and ran out here. Did she hit you?"

"No, Mama, she didn't hit me. I just wanted to say goodbye to Jimmy Lee." Over my shoulder I looked past his mother and glimpsed the final expression of devastation on my friend's face before he disappeared behind their gate.

"Keep your boy away from my child or there's going to be trouble for him." Jimmy Lee's mother stood transfixed, pointing at us.

Mom focused on her as she enfolded me in a protective embrace. In a voice loud enough to be heard, she said, "I know how much you and Jimmy Lee want to play together. But I have told you repeatedly, Eighth Street is a White-only street. This alley divides their world from ours on Church Street. Let's pray that one day white skinned folk and black skinned folk won't impose a skin color divide on their children." She held my face between her hands and continued, "Can you smile for me now, William? Tell me why I shouldn't spank your eight-year-old behind for lying to me about where you were going?"

"I'm sorry, Mama. I just had to say goodbye to Jimmy Lee. I'm sorry." I laid my head on her shoulder, my face pressed against soft golden brown skin, and sobbed deeply. She stroked my head, knelt there in the alley as if we were the only two people in the world. Her gentle hands moving slowly across my back made everything all right.

* * *

To open my senior season of basketball at UCLA,

Coach John Wooden scheduled two games in Provo, Utah, against Brigham Young University. My teammate Conrad and I decided to take a walk to allow our pre-game meal to settle. We obviously presented a stark contrast to the gawking, curious and smiling people we passed.

"How tall are you guys, anyway?" an elderly gentleman and his wife asked. He exaggerated his look up at us in a humorous gesture.

"We're both 6'7", sir," Conrad answered.

Willie and Conrad

"You guys look like you're in the military – butch haircuts and all. You could be brothers, except you're different colors." He held my hand in his, carefully perused my features, mumbled something to his wife, then released me from his scrutiny. We continued our walk.

"Can you believe that guy? That bother you, Naulls?"

"Did you ever think maybe he's never been up close and personal with a black-skinned man before? I was taught that a White man's crude insensitivity is his problem, not mine."

Conrad ingested Mom's wisdom before he thought to ponder what he had swallowed. "Yeah! That applies to all people, right? Right!"

The smell of fresh bread displayed in the window of a quaint mom-and-pop bakery interrupted our introspection. We debated briefly about buying a cinnamon roll but decided not to undermine our purpose in coming to Provo.

"This is the most beautiful place I've ever been. Check out those snow-covered mountains. Look at that cloudless blue sky. And what about these people? They are ostensibly happy with each other. I'm really impressed. What do you think, Conrad?"

"Yeah, me too. I was offered a scholarship here." He paused. "You couldn't go to this school." His eyes clouded with discomfort.

"That, my friend, puts this town and these people in proper perspective." I searched his Nordic features to discern a reaction.

"What?" he innocently shrugged.

Two men and a woman walked directly toward me, interrupting my gait. "William D, do you remember me? I'm Jimmy Lee."

"Jimmy Lee, sure I remember you." He was still a head shorter, but I recognized the face and smile behind his circular, steel framed glasses. "I'm shocked! How have you been and what are you doing here?" Our eyes locked momentarily in search of precious potential. Nothing!

"These are my parents. Dad's a professor here, and I just got back from a student missions trip."

"This is Conrad, my teammate." They nodded acknowledgment as we all scanned each other's faces.

The woman's visage looked like that memorable frown, now turned upside down. How could I ever forget her? Over the years I wondered whether she had sensed the wrath beyond the invisible line of tolerance my mother had drawn that day in the alley. I had never seen the man holding her hand during the time we lived near these Texas fear brokers. Jimmy Lee's father advanced toward me. Looking up into my eyes, he stopped about a foot from my face. Through breath smelling of chocolate covered peanuts, he blurted out, "William D – that's how Jim has referred to you over the years – I'm sorry for the way we treated you." He tightened his grip on my hand, hesitated, cleared his throat and wiped his eyes. "That was a cruel and shameful time in our lives. We're Christians now and know better. Will you forgive us?"

The family encircled me with their arms, prayerfully lamenting in earnest repentance. I was dumfounded, as was Conrad. Composure was restored when Jimmy Lee's fiancée appeared.

Our trainer, Ducky Drake, strolled up and was taken aback by the emotional scene. "Is everything all right, Willie? Hello – all of you. I'm Ducky, UCLA's trainer."

Elvin C. "Ducky" Drake
UCLA Athletic Trainer

Jimmy Lee's mother, tears in full stream, interrupted my response. "Twelve years ago, we lived on the street behind William and his family in Dallas. From the local newspaper we knew he played for UCLA and would be in town. We went to the hotel to look him up to tell him how sorry we are for the awful, demeaning names we called him. He and our son, Jimmy Lee, wanted to be friends when they were young." She turned to redirect attention to me. Her tormented face and body language triggered a momentary quake of empathy. She clutched my hand tightly and said, "William D, please – can you forgive us? Can your mother ever forgive me?"

We embraced again as I reassured them. "Mama had forgiven you by the time we left that alley." Oops! The devil lost another round to Mom's faith.

A puzzled look on his face, Ducky walked away with a growl. "You two, be back in your rooms, off your feet, in fifteen minutes. We got a game to play tonight. Nice meeting you folks."

I never saw Jimmy Lee nor his parents after that day. He and I communicated periodically during his doctoral studies. But – the brief encounter couldn't fill the void of our aborted childhood freedom. The innocence and purity of intent of our fledgling kindred spirits had been maimed, the spine of our bond shattered, back there in the alley.

Maybe God reunited us twelve years later so Jimmy Lee's parents could know that Mom forgave them, even as He did, so they could embrace His Peace. Mom's prayer was fulfilled that day, as Jimmy Lee's parents had learned to look beyond our physical characteristics, at the heart, as God does.

March on Washington • 1963

Right Must Stand In The Patience Of Justice

On a hill far removed, stood a Faith, as sure as the Cross.
The Justice in His Heart could not suffer loss.
And where are they, whose backs so strong as not to sway,
until their strength of Purpose would launch a better way?
That all of us who come behind as life beyond their grave,
could better know their courage strong as food we will to crave.
Three score and three was time when century did record,
Nineteen hundred-plus of years at least did satan stand his guard.
But God sent His Son especially to stop the works of him,
whom we were told to resist after yielding ourselves to Them.
So now, in retrospect, we do look for the fruits,
the acts of those whose Faith in God does witness to recruits.

When the Going Gets Tough . . . .

In the EYE of the hearts of those who care,
and through their confession they might dare
to get going, when pressure to be
is not so popular for their group to see
And over the course of Faith's literacy test,
when given the choice to be God's best,
only through decision can in performance we view
what comes forth in the clutch that our hearts
foreknew

Hidden behind the fear cloaked in expression
is a duplicity of voice of inner complexion
"Judgment is mine," said our Lord so clear
"Learn of Me for your cross to bear"
When the going gets tough, take the route God
points;
Get to going in the Promise on the Way He
anoints

". . . The Tough Get Going"

"You got in."

I couldn't believe what I was hearing. An opportunity to sing with a professional choir and tour all over the United States and Europe. It was a group I hadn't heard of until my voice instructor told me about their reputation. The Coralettes, named for Coral University, had a longstanding tradition in African-American spirituals. Coming from a classically trained background that focused on European arias, I was embarrassed to admit I'd never heard of the group before. But I was so excited I could hardly stand it. I thought, *Maybe I am cut out to be a professional singer. Maybe I am good enough. At least the folks in this group think so.* My voice teacher seemed to think I was ready too.

"That's great; what an incredible break! You'll have to drop about 30 pounds, though; otherwise you're not going to have the stamina." Marni was a blunt woman. Didn't mince words. I tried not to have my balloon deflated this early in the game.

"Yeah, I guess. I thought my audition was really strong. It was probably the hardest I ever had to endure."

Marni sat back in her beige recliner frayed by years of buttock abuse. My mind smiled a thought: *If it could, I bet that chair would fling itself out of the window what with all the vocal warm-ups, high c's, and opera diva wanna be's it had weathered.* Marni was the best voice teacher in West Los Angeles. Even though she was an opera singer – her career peaking in the '60s with an acclaimed performance opposite Domingo at La Scala – she had become a chain smoker. She swore she'd quit, perpetually stubbing out what she claimed was her last Benson & Hedges. I endured the swirls of smoke weekly. She was that good.

"Oh, really. What did you have to do?"

"Well, there was sight reading, I had to sing an aria, and a spiritual; there was ear testing. And then I had to harmonize with a couple of other folks auditioning. And then we had to do a little choreography."

"I told you this group does everything. They don't just stand there like your average zombie choir. You gotta be able to pat your head and rub your belly at the same time."

* * *

"Five minutes to stage."

I put on the finishing touches of my makeup, donned my black sparkly float and headed upstairs toward the stage. I like to be one of the first waiting in the wings. I had a routine of doing five jumping jacks, and five exhalations in quick succession; then I inhale once, slowly and deeply—not too different from how women breathe when giving birth. It was my attempt to diffuse excess nervous energy. We'd been singing this program for months now. Every Saturday afternoon for three hours, we'd woodshed notes, harmonize, learn dance steps. We'd been out on the road and had performed the program now about eight times. But in live performance, every night was an opportunity for "nailing it," or for humiliation. Many times, what made the difference was focus and intent. All my years in athletics had prepped me well for the "stand and deliver" nature of the Coralettes. With each song, someone would step into the spotlight and show the audience what stuff they were made of. Then it was my turn. I stepped out, feeling exposed and vulnerable, chanting in my head almost like a mantra, "Don't bring no weak stuff—no weak stuff."

Charging down the basketball court, dribbling at full speed, my forward trajectory couldn't be stopped. Crowds of high school girls screaming, parents swearing at the refs. Total mayhem in the small community gym. You'd think we were at Madison Square Garden. I think all I heard was a splash of sweat hitting the top of my hand as I pushed the ball forward and down like a machine pounding it into the floor boards. My body felt like liquid, shifting and curving into each opening as I maneuvered down the court. Collecting the ball, I bolted forward in one big rush toward the basket, gathered up my legs and limbs and . . .

Deep River
My home is over Jordan
Deep River Lord
I want to cross over into campground

I was up on the balls of my feet. I wrung the emotion out of each word like a wet cloth, leaving nothing but oxygen to fill my lungs for the next phrase. My body swayed to and fro as if I were in a trance, the "zone" as some refer to it. I had an impulse to take a step forward and speed up the tempo. (I hoped the director would follow.)

Oh don't you want to go
To that gospel feast

With that step I gestured right and caught a glimpse of an old man with a twisted expression on his face. I didn't even catch it full on, just out of my peripheral vision, but it looked like a mix of nausea and vehemence. *Si ma su,* what the hell is this black woman doing, smelling up our new symphony hall?

I gestured left, my gaze following, and met the eyes of a middle aged woman.

Oh that promise lan' that promise lan'

Our eyes locked and I could see tears streaming

down her cheeks, reflective in the stage lights, glimmering like running grunion on a moonlit beach.

Where all is peace
Deep River
My home is over Jordan
Deep River Lord

I began to slow down . . .

I want....to cross...over

Gathering, I gestured upward . . .

Into...

And shot my high A natural out into the ether . . .

Camp ground!

I finished the last note, which hung in the air a second and then dissipated like one of Marni's smoke rings behind the chairs in the balcony. A hushed silence gave way to clapping. Then people started to stand up. I'd sung my best that night – a slam dunk. Each night I picked a different person to sing to who'd gone on to be with the Lord –

Grandma Trent and Lisa, five months
Summer 1965

Grandma Trent; Gommie, my dad's mother; a friend I'd lost in junior high in a plane crash. I sang directly to them, as if we were the only folks in the hall. A small bead of sweat ran down the middle of the back of my neck as I folded into a soft bow. I made sure to glance the way of my curmudgeon, hoping that his disdain had softened. It hadn't. I backed up into my space in the choir curve, acknowledging the director in our momentary communion on stage. I looked out at a packed house. We were in Osaka Symphony Hall in Japan. The audience, so homogeneous from the stage, almost looked like paper doll cutouts strung along the rows of seats.

But that was the moment that God had given me to send His message. He'd given me a voice that night. Most of the audience didn't speak English. And yet there was the unspoken language of God's spiritual world. Through the confines of the Coralette Choir and a singing ex-athlete, the Holy Spirit had given way to boundlessness, both convicting and exposing.

As we signed autographs in the lobby, the woman who had been moved to tears muscled her way to my spot at the table. "Sticky, Sticky" is all she could say, her eyes welling once again.

Our impresario leaned over to me and whispered, "That is Japanese for excellent. It was excellent."

Oh Lord, our Lord, how excellent is Thy name in all the earth. It felt just like making the shot to win a championship game. And we may have in fact won one for the team.

Phony Baloney

Just recently, in a voice so clear
loud enough that my heart did hear, God said,
"Much of your life, you've been a phony,
grieving your righteous soul, you're full of baloney"

. . . .

As a messenger on call of God,
from His throne in heaven above,
I am encouraged that He chastens me
as the expressed faithfulness of His Love
Godly repentance, sewn into Christ's works' deeds
is the path of His harvest, for His in-righteousness seeds
So – most of my life I've been a phony
integrating with people who are full of baloney!

Tact or Deceit?

Good parents often serve as a bench to rest upon. They can be a dependable watering hole on the trek across the deserts of life's journey. Four years had passed since my last refueling stop in Watts. I tossed about anxiously in my old bed in anticipation of our family reunion. The snoring of my two brothers behind the closed door of the next room brought back memories of the Army barracks atmosphere of our youth. Because of my 6′6″ height, the bottom of our six-foot-long stacked bunk beds was assigned to me. My older and younger brothers shared the top bunk. During the winter months a chair was placed to accommodate my blanket-enfolded feet. Our parents' provision had improved dramatically. Now we each had our own bed and they their own rooms, before my return home.

The stage was set for a hero's homecoming that early June day. Mom informed me that neighbors and childhood friends had agreed to gather with our family in honor of the occasion. She emphasized that thanksgiving would be offered up to God for giving me the talent to achieve athletic success. National recognition had come to the Naulls family, San Pedro and the South Central Los Angeles community called Watts.

I pulled back the curtains at the head of the bed to explore the window's view. The white picket fence supported by uniformly spaced red brick pilasters distinguished our property from the neighbors'. *The Thompson boys across the street are both state track champions. Mr. and Mrs. Thompson must be proud. I wonder how the family is doing and whether they will come today?* Alvaro Street, lined with previously owned cars, had no human movement at five-thirty that Saturday morning.

The trek through my brothers' room to the kitchen door was tedious but didn't disturb their slumber. As I stood in the kitchen I could see through the window over the sink beyond Mom's hand-crafted curtains into the back yard's patio and grassy area. I glanced over to the refrigerator on my right and smiled. How many times had I opened that door for delicious leftovers to relieve my hunger pangs? The living room at my left held fond memories too. Very little had changed. The coffee table in front of the couch on the far wall was my study desk on the rare occasions I came home from college for a weekend. The condition of our home appeared decent and in order, a favorite confession of Mom. The carpet and interior walls were in her favorite soft earth tones. The black and white checkerboard tiled floor in the kitchen sparkled as if I, as a part of my weekly chores, had cleaned it an hour before. Mom was still the best homemaker I knew.

I heard movement out front and went to the living room window to check. It was our neighbor placing a package on the porch. I opened the door.

"Good morning, Mr. Martinez. What are you doing up so early?"

"My family wanted to give you this gift in honor of all you have done for our community. We can't make it today because of a previous commitment to visit my mom and dad in San Diego ."

I took the gift and extended my hand. "Thank you very much. You have a safe trip and give our best to everyone."

He turned and stepped off the porch onto the pathway through our front gate. Their family had moved in the month of my departure for UCLA. My mother told me his five children were quiet and mannerable. I inspected the grassy area inside the fence. The edging job from the left boundary to the southern end was perfect. Thick lush Kentucky Bluegrass covered our front yard. Dad's old Pontiac was parked in the driveway next to the fence that divided the properties.

I noticed Eduardo's wife as she walked to their car on the street. "Hello, Mrs. Martinez. How are you?"

"Just fine, Willie. Congratulations on going to college and doing so well. We're proud of you."

"Thank you, Ma'am. Have a safe trip to San Diego." They drove off waving and smiling. There was no other movement on the street. The sky was California gloomy. *Common for the time of year,* I thought. Watts was on hold so I went back inside to prepare for my big day.

"You don't drink coffee, do you, William? Would you like a cup of tea?" Mom was up and ready to serve.

"Good morning, Mom." We embraced. "I'll have some tea. Thank you." We spent some quiet time together rekindling our special bond.

"Today is family and friends giving thanksgiving to God for all His blessings. He has really blessed you, William."

I didn't know what to say, so I nodded.

Later that day, relatives and friends from California and Texas smiled and patted my back in demonstration of family and racial pride.

"Boy, you sure grew up and did big things for a country boy from Texas." My Uncle Million beamed. Those within earshot chuckled in humorous unison.

Two friends from the neighborhood stood at a distance. I attempted to establish eye contact over the flood of relatives but only succeeded in glancing peripheral exchanges. They promised to call and invite me to "come by soon" as they departed.

"You did great, Bro Naulls. If you get a chance, come on by the house and meet my new son. We have two boys and a girl now." TJ, an outstanding athlete, had married his pregnant girlfriend before we graduated from high school.

I said, "Sure, man. Give my best to your family."

"Did you get your degree, William?"

"What are you going to do now, William?"

"Will they help you get a good job, William?"

"Will you play professional ball, William?"

My relatives' relentless inquiry challenged me to face reality. The aftermath of yesterday's glory can serve a purpose. Self-confrontation.

"William, I think it important that you thank everyone for coming."

"OK, Mom."

When everyone's attention had been harnessed, I spoke. "Thank you all for taking the time to come to wish me well. Your interest in my future is important to me. I worked hard to become the 'somebody' people baited me with since I was a little boy in Dallas. My family – which includes all of you – is an integral part of the good things that have happened in my life. Your kind words and many questions encourage me." My dad dried his eyes during the extended applause, a rare spectacle.

I pondered the web of lies I had conjured up to disguise the lack of direction their questions made evident to me. Aunt Eva Mae's tears and Uncle John's fears were seductive. They recounted the segregated south's restraint on family members who were left behind in Texas. "We're so proud that you made good use of your opportunities, son. Many Black people have sacrificed their lives that you might have the freedom to go to college with White folk," Uncle John added.

"Hello, Aunt Rosa and Uncle Elmer. It's good to see you. It's been a long time." Our hugs felt like depth and sincerity.

"Almost thirteen years, William. Our food bill went way down when you left town with your mama." Uncle arched backward, bending his knees to bring forth a roar of laughter. Aunt Rosa's high pitched voice and their joy were infectious and encouraged me to laugh louder and longer. Beautiful olive brown skin, crowned by thick black and white speckled hair and eyebrows gave them a regal appearance. Their wide brown eyes beamed to spread joy. I stood between them as they looked upward to demand my attention and talked about their recollection of my childhood. We became the focus of attention and made it easier for others to join in the fellowship.

I seized the moment to share my heart. "Since our move to California I've longed to have relatives near. Dad and Mom pioneered the move out of Texas, sacrificing closeness to our families. I've heard Mom say that when families strive together for survival and common goals, it spawns unity." Integration was expensive for our generation. I prayed that the price paid of losing family identification was worth the foundation laid for upward mobility and better opportunities for young Black people.

Mom's grip around my arm tightened. The circulation strained. "I love having you back home, honey," she smiled up to me. We strolled together toward the front door to say goodbye to the remaining guests.

"Don't forget to come visit us in Texas," Aunt Rosa whispered in my ear as we hugged goodbye. "Your mother has always really loved you, you know?" Her fixed gaze snatched my attention to a brief retrospective of Mom's commitment to serve my life.

"I know. Thanks for reminding me. I love you, Aunt Rosa."

Each face that passed before me loomed as a painful goodbye. I longed to be able to spend more time with my extended family.

I pined to tell the truth. Sports' demand on my time and mind was on the brink of being unmanageable. I fantasized about going back to college as a non-athlete. That idea grew in intensity during encounters with classmates who had made definite plans for professional pursuits. Basketball was my game, not only in name. It was what I had prepared to be: a consensus All-American and "the best player I've ever seen," according to Coach Wooden's declaration. So what? I thought. I was, after all is said and done, yesterday's headlines. The NBA was a step above the Amateur Athletic Union at that time. In my mind athletic hero status was not subjective. I earned it so there was no sense of failure in my thoughts. In that power frame of mind, I meditated on what to do with the rest of my life.

Mom and Dad would have been crushed had I followed the impulse to share my heart. From their perspective, I had pulled the Naulls name up from scorned shame by the laces of my sneakers into respectability. Mom's lessons struggled forth in my mind. "William, put the truth on a lie every minute because a lie left unchecked is still powerful. There is a reality in truth. It doesn't change."

I abruptly sat up in bed drenched in perspiration. I looked around. Nothing was happening. All that family unity stuff was just my wish and hope in fantasy land. What had been vivid reality a moment before was just an elaborate dream. It was all a dream. I couldn't believe it. Reality set in – there was no hero's welcome for me at my home in Watts. As a matter of fact, my relatives didn't call or write. I lay back on my pillow, wiped my eyes, cleared my mind.

The words of my dream were those of UCLA families at the final awards banquet. My brothers were not in the next room asleep. They didn't live there any more. *It's OK with me,* I thought. The distance between Watts and UCLA stretched some more. *I prefer my space outside this place,* somebody whispered to my mind. *I will not allow family ties to fence me in.*

I turned and sat on the side of the bed to a sobering reality: My parents had paid my major bills through high school; UCLA paid the same for four years of college. Now what – or who? I strolled into the kitchen, pulled out a chair and sat down at the small breakfast table to ponder my options. A pad and pen lay there from my previous late night recording of important thoughts. "What do I do now?" was the question posed at the top of the page. Total assets: $876 in cash, an abused 1953 Mercury Monterey with a purchase contract not fully paid off, some articles of clothing, and lots of trophies and awards. *Is this a respectable bottom line, after four years of university experience?* I pondered. I had no job offers from UCLA alumni or any others, and no college degree. A proposal had come from the Harlem Globetrotters, but I disregarded it. "I'm nobody's clown!" my ego declared to the press.

Coach Wooden had offered that the Athletic Department would pay for completion of my education if and when I chose to pursue that option. Maybe he would take me on as his first African-American assistant? The subject had never been broached. He did say, "Willie is the best player I've ever seen." But did he trust my capacities to teach his players the Wooden philosophy of life? The thought sparked hope. To become a university graduate or even a Ph.D. phoenixed from self-imposed hibernation. At the top of my new "To Do" list, I penned: Call Coach Wooden.

The telephone rang, interrupting the moment. It was Bill Russell, my former nemesis from the University of San Francisco. He said, "Were you sleeping, Westwood?"

"No, but my family is."

"Good." His loud, infectious laughter that followed cleared out my eardrums. "I want you to come and play basketball with our national championship team on a tour of Central and South America. The U.S. State Department is footing the bill, so it's like a two-month first-class paid vacation. What do you say, Westwood Willie?"

"Have you notified Coach Wooden and UCLA?" I was so accustomed to getting Coach's permission to do anything that my mind's automatic response asked the obvious question.

Bill, in his quickest wit, shot back, "How much eligibility you got left, Westwood?" Then he roared in laughter again.

Slightly embarrassed by the naïveté of the question, I mumbled, "Zero and counting."

Fifteen minutes of friendly persuasion later, I agreed to join the NCAA Player of the Year, my biggest rival for athletic supremacy in college basketball. What did it mean to be thought of as an honorary ambassador of the USA to the people of Central and South America? The stated purpose was to spread America's Good Will. Dare we tell the truth about racial and socioeconomic conditions at home in America?

Mom's voice echoed again from my soul's bank: "William, if you don't have anything good to say, don't say anything at all."

She's right again, responded my soul to my heart.

Hmm-m-m-m. In my dream and now in this decision I had agreed mentally to be sensitive and tactful at the expense of my heart's truth. Was it a web of deceit weaving itself in the guise of pleasing and not offending others? What about sage wisdom, which says, "To thine own self be true"?

I was challenged in deep thought about my future for the first time in life. Students called it the "weight of choice." To choose the right path was heavy stuff. My dilemma was whether to prepare for institutional academic certification or step out as an entrepreneur. Mom's wisdom surfaced yet again: "The 'heavy stuff' you young folk talk about is resolved through hard work toward respectable independence. Count your blessings. You have greater opportunities than most Black people in our country's history."

UCLA's professors had promised to prepare me well. "If you commit to academics as you have to basketball, you will be more successful in the long run," Mrs. Savage, my counselor, had advised.

After a few days of meditation on my options, I concluded that my heart still belonged to basketball. I decided to pursue and live life to its fullest expression through my athletic talent – for pay. That was the final answer to my dilemma. "One's best athletic expression," said a wise observer, "comes through prepared, unrelenting mental and physical pursuit of excellence, when body and mind are most productive. It is a short run goal."

I determined that I would put on hold a long run goal to sit at the feet of UCLA's academic best. When my body told me, "That's enough, Willie," I would return.

Indecision's Cooing

© 2005 William D. Naulls

What to do
when ceremoniously through
used up and finished
value to all – diminished
no life-long goals established
finished!
God's Voice emerged:
Carry on from here
Be still, listen
Let your head clear
Fruit is of your planting 'til now
Sow in better ground to plow
You've walked on your own for years
No profit comes through fears
Gather the weeds – bundle them to burn
Kick the dust off your heels,
to My Seed planted turn

Spiritual Crossroads

When the time came to negotiate a contract with a professional basketball team, I sought the advice of my beloved Coach John Wooden. He was reputed to be a man of God and prayer. There was an awe thing that came upon me whenever I entered into his presence, like being a little boy again. He knew the purpose of my visit yet appeared bothered, as though I put him in an uncomfortable position. There he sat, arms folded, with a puzzled look on his face, apparently thinking, *What does he want me to be – a negotiating advantage?*

John R. Wooden
UCLA Head Basketball Coach, Emeritus

To relieve the tension, I blurted out, "What do you think I should ask for as compensation for my services."

"Take whatever they offer you and be grateful." His eyes pierced my soul. He continued to unleash. "I remember my first contract negotiation. Don't get a reputation for being greedy." His answer was the same advice he had been given after college by his coach/advisor: "Take whatever they offer you and be grateful."

I sat stunned, my mouth and eyes wide open in silence. He appeared prideful that his advisor had instructed him to let the team owners fill in an amount for his value to them. An eerie, familiar feeling surfaced. I remembered similar advice from my mother during negotiations for my athletic scholarship: "Go to the university you really want to attend, not where you think you can get the most for playing basketball. I'm praying that you choose a coach who will teach you principles to develop character to make right decisions."

On the way back to my car I shrieked out loud in sarcastic laughter. "Take whatever they offer? How could Coach be so naïve?" I screamed, flailing my arms toward heaven. "Contract negotiations for services rarely look out for the proletariat. Value to any prospective employer must be negotiated using the laws governing supply and demand," I regurgitated. UCLA professors had taught me that conclusion.

A cluster of students heard my emotional outburst. They seemed concerned. "Is everything OK, Willie?"

Somewhat embarrassed, I moved a step away, allowing space for a campus hero's response. "I'm fine. Thanks for asking." The finality in my tone dismissed their puzzled faces as I turned and walked away.

I left the campus that day with a sage lesson. If I were looking for basketball advice, Coach Wooden was the man. But when making a decision about contract negotiations, I had to be mindful to choose an advisor who had knowledge specific to the area of my need. That lesson became foundational in my life's journey.

What were NBA players paid? I didn't know, but soon found out that salaries were well kept secrets. Today one can search the Web to discover the annual salary of most athletes in any sport. Not so at that time. Unwritten rules of engagement dictated by owners conspired secretly to prohibit the disclosure of contract details. A violation was grounds for a player's release. Recent research has disclosed that black skinned athletes were paid much less than their white skinned counterparts.

I was entering into a unique kind of slave market, an evil system of greed. All skin colors were included, but the principle of management's obsession to control the cost of labor was intact. Coach had to know that, didn't he? It suddenly dawned on me that he did not live by laws impacting business negotiations. How could a man be so competitive in sports yet have no apparent concern about what he was worth in the open marketplace? How could he not be concerned about what his employer determined to pay him? I am an All-American witness from the foundation of his UCLA legacy. He, ostensibly, has never been the least bit concerned about money.

I was not forced to enter the professional basketball marketplace. It was my choice. Few Blacks before me were so blessed with the privilege of choice. By choosing to participate, I determined that I had to learn to master negotiating techniques for my salary. I developed a comfort zone with those thoughts. The integrated classrooms of my university experience liberated me from fear of whom I was perceived to be. But Coach's advice puzzled me. His image surfaced in my mind during many contract negotiations during professional basketball, business and contract negotiation careers.

Coach retired after winning a record ten national titles. A writer for a national publication reported, "Rival NCAA coaches resent what they perceive to be John Wooden's naïve approach to contract negotiations. They blame him in unofficial complaints for their low salaries."

The athletic directors' association, in response to disgruntled coaches, were reported to have said, "Coach Wooden of UCLA continues to win national basketball championships. His annual salary has never exceeded $35,000. Each year he sends his signed one-year contract back to the athletic office with the space for salary amount blank. The obvious conclusion is he loves what he is doing and leaves salary details up to the discretion of Athletic Director J. D. Morgan's conscience."

Today, at 99 years mature, Coach Wooden continues to be guided by his inner Counselor to live in God's peace and prosperity. The fruit of his choices is evident. He has been honored and rewarded financially in more abundance in his latter years than ever and has not strayed because of criticism for his choices.

Mom's prayer that I would "choose a coach" who would influence me to develop into a man of Godly character was answered. Coach Wooden's example conveyed to me that doing what God commands is more important than how much financial benefit is offered for my efforts. When I responded to the call to God's ministry I was encouraged by the wisdom in Coach's counsel.

The Spiritual Crossroads of Faith

Two contending forces
co-dwell within my sphere
one's hidden agenda
makes the Other One's clear
for He comes giving Love
His enemy sells hate
Which I yield to and serve
will determine my fate

Every Child Is Our Child

Parents' Wail to Children

How can we shield you from hurt and pain
Field every heartache in our strength to drain?
Be the solution to each problem you face
Shoulder the burden of your every race?

. . . .

God to Parents and Children

I AM LOVE to relieve the hurt in your pain
Let Me rid you of heartache, in MY STRENGTH
to drain
I AM the solution to every problem you face
MY SON shoulders your burden in the thick of
each race

From Russia to Love

It was a hot day in late August, 2004. George sensed anxiety as Kathy's grip tightened. He had experienced pre-game jitters many times during his illustrious athletic career at Syracuse University and a professional stint in the NBA and Europe. But this situation was clearly out of his power to control.

Kathy moved toward the information kiosk of the Austin, Texas, airport. "I'm going over to check the flight arrival schedule again. I'll be right back." She was still attracted to George after 25 years. Without the long blond hair, platform shoes, necklace and tight bell-bottomed jeans he had worn when she first met him, he remained her George. His former life had gone by the wayside. After he ceased being the manager of Rick "Superfreak" James and left the profession when trust was violated, he pursued several options before finding his true calling.

George focused his gaze into her green eyes and gradually opened up the lock of his concern for her peace. "OK," he said as he watched her walk away.

Thoughts raced as he recalled their first meeting at Gelson's Market in Century City, a suburb of Los Angeles. Her stately movement snared his once-in-a-lifetime attraction, releasing in his mind that first feast on her gentle gait up the parking lot ramp. The momentary trance aside, his lips moved slightly to murmur in an unheard whisper, "She's still got the longest and best looking legs of all time." His head tilted slyly to the left as a grin of lust formed.

Was it fate that caused their paths to cross that day? What are the odds of a California girl, born in Santa Monica near the Pacific Ocean and educated at

Beverly Hills High School, yoking up with an upstate New York, cocky graduate of Ten Broek Academy in the small village of Franklinville? There is only one explanation: With God, all things are possible.

* * *

George and Kathy have everything Americans work for and dream to achieve: wisdom, humility, wealth, health and upward mobility. A high achieving and honored industrial real estate investor and deal maker for over thirty-five years, George has earned the reputation of one who undergirds his common sense with good sense, both within and outside the business community. His ethics are praised as impeccable. The modest 3500 square foot home in Bel Air where they have lived for over thirty years camouflages their socioeconomic status. Only through an examination of their philanthropic generosity can one begin to grasp the full measure of their financial empire. George has owned race horses for years and is the founder/CEO of Cardinal Industrial. He and Kathy spend a great deal of their time traveling around the world – to Africa, India, Russia, Japan, Turkey, China, and the Middle East. They love and prefer each other over any others. Their casual lifestyle is the envy of many, and friends who knew them well were unaware that not having children had become an important issue.

George's booming voice pierced the tranquility of Kathy's reading environment in the family room overlooking the Pacific Ocean in the distance. "What's gonna happen when my father dies – and I die? I don't have any cousins or uncles; nobody in the Hicker line is left but Dad, Mom and me."

Kathy walked through the double doors into the living room and across to George, who sat in his favorite reclining chair in front of a wide-screen television. "What are you thinking, George? This is the second time you've mentioned wanting kids. I'm not a young woman any longer, you know!"

A slight smile curled the right side of his mouth. "Might be fun to try, my little honey-bunny."

They embraced in agreement.

Two years later, doctors suggested *in vitro* fertilization. After an unproductive period in that direction, the prospect of using a surrogate mother was considered but rejected by various agencies. "You're past the age for us to recommend that as a positive alternative. Why don't you go home and rethink where you are in life. You are both over forty now, aren't you?"

That night in bed, Kathy sobbed. "I've let you down, George. I should have thought of bearing children for you when I was young. I'm so sorry."

Kathy rested her head on his chest and he gently stroked her long blonde hair. "You didn't let me down. I never thought of having kids before. I was happy not sharing you with anyone. If either of us should be called selfish, it's me. I'm the one who waited all these years to ask you to bear me an heir. Please don't blame yourself."

They drew nearer in spiritual submission of their souls one to the other. Since he first knew her, George had given up, piece by piece, his mountain of macho. He strove to be the man she would cleave to in such a time as this. "It's not your fault. Please don't be sad. We can adopt an older child so the subject of nursing and infant care is not an issue."

"Oh, George. Thank you for always being where I need you, whenever I need you. I love you."

"Me, too. We'll start anew tomorrow. We'll find the child that God has chosen for us. So far, I've not concentrated on prayer or casting all our cares on God. He cares for us and will grant us all our desires and needs according to His riches in glory by Christ Jesus."

"George, you sound like our friend, Preachin' Willie!"

They laughed out loud.

"My brother does come on strong at times. But we need God's intervention now. We've done all we can do, so let's agree to trust in the Lord with all our hearts, and not lean on our own understanding. The Bible tells us to acknowledge the Lord in all our ways, and He will direct our path. Agreed?"

"OK, George. Whatever you decide, I will support with all my heart."

He wiped the tears from her cheeks and kissed her lips gently. "Go to sleep now, sweetheart."

Initially frustrated by America's insensitive adoption system, George and Kathy nevertheless continued to investigate. They spent time with and considered adopting a brother and sister, aged nine and seven respectively, only to find them to be unmanageable, lacking in self control and discipline. Both had been born to a crack cocaine user and had floundered in foster care. The Hickers learned that the most unreasonable expectation of the adoption system here in our country is the requirement that a couple commit to a child without sufficient time to bond. Simply put, when a couple chooses a child, that child is not allowed to live in their home environment for a reasonable amount of time in order for the child and family to become acquainted. Therefore the couple is unable to make an informed decision about adoption. The system's plan appears to focus on getting rid of children rather than placing each where there is a unique "fit" within a positive home environment.

George and Kathy spent thousands of dollars and many heart wrenching hours pursuing their hope. They had choices: Stop the search and do nothing more, or continue to trust in the Lord to give them the desire of their hearts, that special child.

Out of the silence of faith, Randi Thompson and Chris Reid of Kidsave spoke forth hope. "Why don't you adopt a Russian child? Have you heard of Children's Hope International? We have a contact. Would you like their number?"

Kathy called George immediately. "Guess what just happened!"

"The Cardinals fired Tony LaRussa?"

"Be serious, George! Why is the first thing that comes to your mind Cardinals baseball or Syracuse basketball?"

"OK. What happened?"

"In a casual conversation today someone referred us to a group that encourages and assists in the adoption of kids from China, Russia, Eastern Europe and South America. We can see pictures and select the one we're interested in."

"That's good news. Let's get on it. What do we do?"

"They will call us soon."

"Good news. I'll call you on my cell on my way home from the office."

They met with Randi of Kidsave who encouraged them to consider adopting a child from another country. In March of 2004 George and Kathy were shown pictures of sixty orphaned Russian children. George selected the pictures of a thirteen year old nicknamed Kolya and his eleven year old brother, Kostya.

"We'll take them both!" George offered.

Their scheduled arrival five months later encouraged their faith that God does hear and answer prayers.

* * *

"The plane lands in fifteen minutes." Kathy was back, looking at George like a five year old child ogling candles on her birthday cake.

This was the beginning of a six week period of making decisions. The boys' guest stay at the Hickers' home back in Bel Air, California, was critical. George, always in self control, appeared uneasy, a little unsettled. *We've waited so long,* he thought. *This could be our last shot.* He mumbled a private prayer. *God, you are the producer and director of this situation. Even though we've not met these boys, I sense a peace in my uneasiness. I trust you, Lord. You know the desires of our hearts. I trust you, Lord.*

Fourteen Russian children walked into the terminal earlier than scheduled. From the photo supplied by Kidsave, George and Kathy spotted the two brothers they had chosen to host for a six week "trial fit." An interpreter from Kidsave introduced the four prospects to each other. George immediately liked what he saw. The boys had his blond hair and enough other similar physical characteristics to engage his mind. Kathy sensed the love of a spiritual birth mother.

"George and Kathy, this is Kostya and Kolya."

Kostya and Kolya
August 2006

Their frail bodies, undersized by American standards for thirteen- and eleven-year-old boys, didn't appear to matter as the four left the terminal. No one said much, but gestures sufficed. George and Kathy knew immediately. These boys would be Hickers. The road map was unclear, but they settled in as God's co-pilots. They trusted in Him to direct their path. The boys were unaware that they were being considered for adoption. Kidsave had only let them know that they were on an extended vacation hosted by an American couple. The agency's sensible policy allowed a six week trial period to determine whether a comfort zone would establish its foundation in the hearts of these strangers.

The airplane ride from Austin to Los Angeles was uncomfortable but uneventful. Although communication was strained, the boys seemed undaunted, especially given their previous twelve hour flight on Aeroflot from Moscow to Houston and their subsequent flight to Austin. Two bilingual dictionaries kept the kids and prospective parents on their toes during the whirlwind tour of the Hicker world.

The boys' time in California was filled with new experiences. They spent time at a camp that included other Russian children as well as time alone with George and Kathy on various trips. By the end of their stay, the Hickers had determined to adopt Kolya and Kostya, although they were advised not to tell the boys their plans because many hurdles were ahead in the lengthy and complicated adoption process. A change in leadership of the Russian Ministry of Education and adoption bureaucracy delayed that process and necessitated duplication of the masses of paperwork, but George and Kathy persevered.

* * *

Kathy awakened at the thump of rubber tires meeting the runway of Moscow International Airport. In December 2005, she had decided to visit the orphanage by herself to celebrate Kolya's fifteenth birthday and to reassure the boys of their love and intention to bring them to America. A quick glance toward the awakening passengers in the next seats relieved her insecurity of not having George at her side. The elderly man held his wife's hand firmly, unaware that his snoring had made it difficult for Kathy to fall asleep.

"Did you have a pleasant sleep, young lady?"

Kathy nodded. "And you?"

The flight attendant announced the arrival at the terminal. Kathy's thoughts shifted. *I still have a long trip overland to get to the boys. Staying overnight here is a wise decision, but I'd rather be there as soon as possible.*

A man with her name on a sign caught her eye as she walked up the ramp into the terminal. "Mrs. Hicker, Children's Hope International arranged for me to drive you to the hotel. Tomorrow morning, I will come for you at nine to take you to Smolensk, about a 250 mile drive to the west."

As the driver maneuvered through the crowded and disorganized traffic flow, Kathy was enthralled by the beautiful array of swirling colors and redbrick towers of St. Basil's Cathedral. She longed to have the time to explore its nine individual chapels, each topped with a unique onion dome, but that would have to await a different trip.

"Is there a good restaurant near the hotel that you recommend?"

"We have several for you to choose from. I will get the list and someone will escort you to wherever you wish to go."

"Thank you."

That night, she ventured out into the bitter cold

to get some borscht before settling down.

Kathy slept well in spite of the inadequately heated hotel room. She awakened early, eager to continue her mission.

"The infrastructure of highways and bridges is maintained quite well," Kathy commented as they drove out of the city the next morning. The driver shrugged his shoulders and grunted acknowledgment.

She marveled at the beautiful open landscape between Moscow and Smolensk.

"Is there a drug problem here?"

He glared at her reflection in the rear view mirror. "There is everything to be bought in Moscow, but there are no drugs out here in the countryside. The orphanage and surrounding communities are drug free. There are simply none around. The authorities are very strict against illegal drug sales."

Kathy's inner glow flushed her face, cooled by the tears of joy that teased to overflow. "That is good news," she said in a tone of optimism.

She had learned that the small village where some of the orphanage personnel lived did not have any accommodations for visitors, so she had made arrangements for a hotel in Smolensk, where she would spend each night of her four-day visit. The nights were difficult as she needed to wear most of her clothes to bed in the unheated hotel room. Fortunately she was able to borrow an appropriately heavy coat from her translator. The designer coat she had brought, though perfect for California, was grossly inadequate for the Russian winter.

Once she had dropped her things at the hotel, she was anxious to get to the orphanage to see Kolya and Kostya. Approximately fifty miles east of Smolensk, the driver turned off the main highway onto a narrow country road. After a few more miles in a wooded area, a beautiful lake was suddenly in full view. The scene brought a smile to Kathy's face. Soon thereafter they were in the midst of a cluster of several three-story cement block and mortar buildings. Inside, the stark hardwood floors and plastered walls were hospital clean. The common restroom facilities were utilitarian, sturdily built of materials used to endure heavy use, and well maintained. She was grateful to see that Kolya and Kostya were not living in poverty, filth or decay as she had feared.

The following days Kathy shared an exhilarating experience in the boys' environment. She learned firsthand that what the average American experiences as bare necessities were luxuries for the children. Adequate and sufficient toilet paper, toothpaste, soap, a change of clothing or underwear – even meat to eat – were as rare as privacy and an appreciation for individuality. It took all of Kathy's strength of mind to maintain emotional composure as she shared the gifts she had brought.

In barely audible thoughts, she murmured from her heart, "You are our boys and we will get you out of here."

The boys looked confused. Her whisper campaign had intended to plant in them a seed of confidence in her. Surprisingly, Kathy found the orphanage to be a place which offered caring companions. Other children with similar backgrounds counteracted the trauma of their father's suicide when Kolya was just two and Kostya was still in his mother's womb, three months from birth. Subsequently, they had survived the abuse of their mother and an alcoholic stepfather who beat and verbally abused all three until the state removed the boys and placed them in the orphanage. They had endured much. Their hope for anything better was seared but given a new perspective of a better life by Kathy's presence and words of encouragement.

The love George sent Kathy to share was Hicker-firm in the Lord. There was no shadow of turning. The boys heard that the Hickers were fully persuaded that God would honor His Word and deliver them together to the promised land.

* * *

In June of 2006, both George and Kathy made the first of two mandatory visits to the orphanage. Two months later, they made a final visit, during which the official adoption took place. Paperwork was completed in Smolensk, updating the boys' Russian passports. A visit to the United States Embassy to procure the required documents ensured they would be able to travel to their new home.

As they had been told by Embassy personnel, the moment the plane landed at Los Angeles International Airport, Kolya and Kostya Hicker officially became American citizens. They all can witness from experience, God is faithful.

Kathy • Kolya • Kostya • George
Christmas 2008

Love's Seed

Love is in the Pit of it all
the Seed – where the residue is so thick
fermenting Passion in the heart to beat quick
blending goodness in every season
causing people to smile in everlasting reason
Love's Seed is the Pit of it all
there an enemy forgives generational foes
forestalling current and future woes
Love's Seed is the Pit of it all

Love's Seed Redefines Priorities

It was fall. The competitive juices' flow of mind and body reminded me of their seasonal habit of intense training. My size-14 feet twitched in resistance to the idleness as I rested among fallen leaves in the leisure of UCLA's upper campus academic environment. I sat totally at peace under a Sycamore tree savoring the freedom of a physically non-competitive world. For the first time in 20 years I hadn't made a commitment to someone else's agenda in sports competition. The California sun flushed my face and arms as a soft Pacific breeze gently dusted past my cheek bones over closed eyelids. My thoughts drifted. As a youth, hands were laid on my head in church to claim freedom of choice: freedom for every person to compete in a world of unlimited opportunities and of equality of human and civil rights. *We've certainly come a long way from Dallas.* I was talking to myself again.

I did not regret putting aside retirement from professional basketball to pursue and win three World Championship rings with the Boston Celtics. But, during that commitment, the thought of living the vision of the Mamas and Papas' "California Dreaming" grew. I pined in anticipation of the day I would enroll and sit on this campus in the sun as a non-athlete. The chatter of students passing by brought a smile to my face. I pondered the difference in the conversations of this college atmosphere compared to those of a pro training camp. What a mental and physical transformation my decision to retire initiated.

The trance was interrupted by the faint sound of little bells clinking against one another. As I opened my eyes, they adjusted slowly to the sunlight. My attention focused in the direction of the sound announcing an oncoming presence. Her shapely form was clothed within a short-short skin-tight mini-dress accentuating long, beautiful legs. Bare feet intensified my curiosity as our eyes, in full focus now, met, challenging our sense of vulnerability. There was an alluring charm in her response to my intercepting course. Hand extended, my emotional craving was far more spiritual than base physical. I smiled an alluring personality forward, "Hello, my name is Willie."

"I'm Anne. Yes, I'd love to" was her reply to my greeting and invitation to join me in California dreaming. Her handshake was as gentle as her soft voice and mirrored the manner in which long artistic fingers caressed the leather sandals at her side. I searched her eyes. An unexpected depth emerged and spilled over into a forbidden and guarded zone. The spiritual hook grabbed hold and challenged, as if to never let me go. I gulped to relieve the anxiety as she approached and passed beyond our comfort zone. On her shoulder hung a large hand-made leather bag. Little bells dangled from its side, responding to movement. The sharp sound, up close now, struck an harmonic chord, an alarm to not allow our encounter to escape further exploration. Head tilted downward to the left, her hand pulled hair aside, uncovering fascinating green eyes, never releasing intensity, as we gracefully descended to the Sycamore's base.

There was a sensed comfort and anticipation in the ease of getting to know each other in the time that was convenient to her class schedule. Who can predict how long is necessary for the seed of love to take root? Hand to hand, shaking *auf wiedersehen* (until we meet again), we parted as serious contenders to be covenant-bearers; my hand touched her back under waist-length hair; her submissive grasp across my bicep conceived our yoke. The parting smile and wave of goodbye over her shoulder encouraged hope to be fulfilled that challenged my will. In less than thirty minutes, a total stranger and I were launched together on a sure course.

As a fish hook lodges deep underneath a muscle concealing its purpose, so our meeting placed Anne deep into my soul's resistance. Attempts to move away only ensnared me deeper and taught me submission to find relief. The thought of a pruned character to be the man this encounter inspired in my heart encouraged a longing I had lived for most of my adult athletic life. Maybe her heart also sensed a need for a meaningful alignment, a mutual commitment of souls. Maybe she also experienced the excitement of inner peace, hope that is energized to trust. Was it her yielding of power in this encounter that made us unique? Why the sudden embrace of what I perceived to be a need to commit my power to bring happiness into her life? I wanted to tell her then, in that space, not to worry or cry alone any more. I'd be there beside her, to blot out and soothe her weeping fears – for the rest of our years. Then she was gone, out of sight, but not out of mind.

During the fulfilling weeks that followed, even as my heart sealed its destiny, I was confused by the pain. Mentally I resisted the persistence of the hook's intensity. For many years I struggled to be free of conviction to never again marry. I was especially concerned with the racial issue of that day. Everywhere we went in any community, we were looked upon with scorn. Anne is of WASP heritage and my soul defied the inner logic of my heart for years. The conflict love introduced influenced reasoning. Black history in this country weighed heavily in my subconscious. The pain of integration continues to be subtly reinforced until this day.

Like a ship's anchor, her love impeded my uncharted mobility at every turn, until my obedience to love's purpose caused the hook's pain to cease to burn. Our relationship's intensity stretched in conflict resolving encounters. We allowed slack to prepare professionally – she in medicine and I in entrepreneurial pursuits – in the while that passed. When the easing tension in the anchor's line evoked a sense of abeyance, we met to assure that we were not going anywhere in life without each other. The line evolved from strength of patient endurance through mental and physical resistance to a strong shared life cord of nurturing love.

Two different cultures we came from, but we committed to Love as our priority culture. The more the world stereotyped us to be, the stronger we lived in God's Word to see. Love's Seed persevered. We united to be one in the other, each being free to live out Spiritual destiny. I love you, Anne.

Willie & Anne • 1967 • Pacific Grove

Once You Find Her . . . .

God says, and I paraphrase:

The man who finds a wife finds a "thing"
that is good
To love as Christ loves the church, he
earnestly should
But he who loses self control yields to
slipping
his gift from God can become contentious
dripping

Once you have found her, you must never
let her go
Show her in every way to conclusively
know
that she's God's gift to you exclusively – so
once you have found her, you must never
let her go

In Loveness

There is a timing, a patience of cadence shared by
In Loveness ones
that is only interrupted when lust, and its false
pledge to trust,
is ingested with another to temporarily see and
touch
an urgency of out of control cavalier relief and such

Consider the rarity of In Loveness, like kind
direction in the hearts of he and she,
fulfilling and bringing to fruition the will of God
for them to be

. . . .

First Love

I fell in love with the bridge of his nose. It was caramel with freckled flecks. It sloped outward, broad and strong. The tip was round and slightly pudgy like it belonged to an eight year old. His nose was a dichotomy of man/boy qualities, both endearing and sweet, rugged and intelligent.

We clinked our Guaranas and took long luxurious swigs. It had been a fun day off, a one day vacation of sorts before we had to get back on the bus and travel ten hours to the next performance city. Touring was grueling, but having respites near Morro de Sao Paolo made it worthwhile.

I felt as comfortable in the crook of his arm as anywhere. We played footsies in our white tube socks that we'd purchased at an open market the day before. Jeff had become my home away from home. I didn't exactly connect with the other performers. They were about as supportive as a pack of rabid dogs terrorizing a kitten up a tree, waiting for it to lose its footing. I tried to figure out why I was so vehemently disliked.

"I don't get it. I'm a good person. A nice person. I try to be helpful."

"That's just it," Jeff quipped. "The more beautiful you are, the more they can't stand you. They can't believe that someone as sweet as you actually exists so they choose to believe that you don't . . . that you're a fraud."

A fraud? I thought. I knew what that meant but was baffled how it could apply to me. If I was nothing else, I was sincere. Often sincerely naïve, sincerely wrong, sincerely stupid – but sincere.

"Do you think I'm fake?"

He nuzzled my neck and pulled me in tight, "No, baby, I know for a fact you're the real deal." His baritone voice was rich and resonant. The backs of my knees started to perspire slightly. I wasn't used to all of this attention. I never consciously avoided men and yet I'd somehow managed to steer clear of them for nearly a decade. I looked on at couples holding hands in the mall, teens necking on shabby blankets in the park, and scratched my noggin in wonderment. It was so foreign to me, I couldn't even be jealous. And then two months after my 30th birthday, I found myself affectionately cornered in a hotel elevator by a tall drink of Malagasy descent .

"Here, let's play a game," Jeff continued. You come up with adjectives that you think describe you and I'll tell you how they translate for our Coralette friends." The Coralettes had been traveling professionally for as long as I'd been alive. Respected in the choral arenas both nationally and internationally, the group had a reputation for being as fierce backstage as it was onstage.

"Ok, let me see . . . umm . . . well, how about friendly."

Jeff fired off, "Needy."

"Ok, then, how about supportive."

"Manipulative." He didn't miss a beat.

"Intelligent."

"Arrogant."

"Shy."

"Stand-off-ish."

"Caring."

He hesitated and flashed a bit of a sly grin. "You mean weak ."

"How do you know? What makes you so sure of yourself?" I asked, my innards working up a little concoction of shock with a hint of hurt. How was he able to come up with them so quickly?

"Look I've grown up with these folks all of my life. Not exactly these folks but they might as well have been. I know 'em like I know my own reflection. Sad but true. It's the result of four hundred years of enslavement." At another time, he would have launched into a Marcus Garvey soliloquy.

Jeff had grown up extremely poor and neglected. He had a drunk womanizer as a father and a mother who was a young promising classical soprano but who'd spent her life on prescription medicine and in assisted living facilities. As a teen, she'd been walking home from her voice lesson and was raped in an alley by two men, then dragged through glass. Her mind was never the same and her future career was annihilated. She managed to bear three children but couldn't care for them, emotionally or otherwise. Jeff was the baby; but the only thing he'd suckled in his life was a bitter cigarette stub. He'd grown up in street combat with a "getting over "attitude, and had become cunning, militant, and seared. Today, though, he picked an oversized wild lily for me and lay it by my place setting at breakfast.

We packed our luggage and loaded up the bus for the umpteenth time. Jeff and I settled in somewhere around the middle row, cuddling up under a huge knit blanket to muffle our whispers and shield our thumb wrestling.

Bus psychology was fit to be studied by the masters. Long time Coralette veteran, Gwen, and the group director always claimed the first two rows. Calvin, the group accompanist, perched himself in the back row, never shifting his Buddha-like position whether he was eating, listening to music or sleeping.

Then there were the rowdies who liked to sit near the back but not too far back as to disturb Calvin's

Buddha chi. Recounting old Coralette stories, trying to remember all of the words to the Gilligan's Island theme song, pointing out shacks on the landscape and yelling out, "That's your house" – all would send the rowdies into uproarious laughter. The rest of the bus would no doubt be annoyed but wouldn't dare say anything for fear of being shunned or labeled uncool.

And then there were the nomads who really didn't have a home seat or row. They just sort of drifted, hoping to latch on to someone else's bus identity.

Being mid-row was a subconscious (or maybe not so subconscious) attempt at Sweden – complete neutrality amidst all traveling factions, acting as bus ombudsman in disputes. Internal beefs could be plotted on a map based on who sat where on the bus. Marian and Laura sat on polar opposites ever since Laura's watch "accidentally" got caught in Marian's weave and pulled half of it out five minutes before performance time.

Tony sat directly in front of me. He'd been performing since grade school and had actually been able to buy his home with the money he'd made from background singing in the '70s. Even though he himself didn't have a name, he'd worked in the biz with some of the greats – Aretha and Ray, to name drop. Never without his Seabreeze astringent, he had a daily bus ritual of swabbing his face, neck and throat until his skin was raw.

Jeff often slept on the bus. It was my opportunity to really study him. I ran my hand down the side of his face and felt the feathery air escape from his nostrils. His breath was deep. The angle of his eyelid suggested Asian descent. Jeff had a little pocket Bible that he carried with him everywhere. The rest of the group scoffed whenever he'd pull it out – at meals, in the backstage dressing room, on the bus. When he read a Psalm, his speaking voice was a snake charmer. Its melody and rhythm lifted me up high and rocked me back and forth like a cradled infant. His recitations often brought me to tears. He stirred a bit, then woke up.

"Why are you crying?" His lips were only inches from my ear. I reached out and scratched lightly the petal of my lily. I'd managed to tuck it in the back fold of the seat in front of me.

"I don't know."

His question was in no way indignant or mocking. It was soft.

I looked up and watched the Portuguese countryside gallop by and could see bull billboards speckled on the belt of the distant horizon.

"I guess I'm happy."

When I think of home
I think of a place where there's love overflowing
I wish I was home
I wish I was back there with the things I been knowing . . . .

* * *

"You're really doing great work, Alicia." I tried to encourage my students as much as possible. With touring over, I'd managed to build a modest little voice studio at home. Alicia may not have sounded like Beverly Sills but who's to say she won't be the next Britney Spears? She handed me a check. "Same time next Thursday?"

"Sounds great. See you then."

"Oh, I forgot to tell you, I saw in the Register that the Coralettes are performing at St. George's Church this weekend."

It was a little late in the evening to muster any feigned enthusiasm. How could she know that the billows in *that* sail had long since deflated.

"Isn't that the group you used to sing with?"

"Yes, it's been a minute, but it's good to hear they're still performing."

Did I really mean that? The years had replaced sincerity with something a bit more smelly.

Ten years had passed since I'd donned my touring gear. The Marians and Tonys had long moved on and the group was dominated by surly yet driven twenty something's with a thirst for musical blood. I missed the performing and getting paid while traveling to different countries, but that was really about all. Most everything else about those touring days had become as worn and faded as an old dish towel – a memory that you threw in the wash over and over again – tattered, but too utilitarian to toss away.

I closed the door behind her and made my way to the back. I heard soft breathing noises and was relieved our vocal ranting hadn't disturbed my little one. I turned off the main light and fumbled through the dark to the other side of the room where the small table lamp sat. Tomorrow I had to work on a couple of songs I'd dug up in my music library for a Saturday audition. This new group which I'd heard about through one of my students weren't the Coralettes but at least I could keep my chops up, maybe get a little performing in, and even earn a little gas money while I was at it.

I bumped my shin against the end of the bed and the deep rhythmic breathing abruptly stopped. "Ssssh, honey, it's just me, baby." My son settled back down and within nanoseconds was once again in the pocket. I lay down on the side of the bed and reached up to feel for the lamp switch. I only turned on the night light so I could watch him even for a moment before I fell unconscious myself. Even though strangers would agree that my son seemed to be a clone of me, I was still surprised at how much he favored Jeff. Those big round orbs with a whisper of heavy lash. Full brown lips slightly parted and curved elegantly at the corners. The one little freckle just above his caramel brow. And his nose. The same brilliant nose that had captivated me ten years earlier.

I let my finger run down his temple, and in his sleep, he giggled. My heart couldn't hold it. The joy crashed as those Sao Paolan waves had years before, and I felt the tears sprout like liquid buds. Jeff had brought me flowers once when his baby was weeks old. I would not see him again. Resting by my son's side, on rare occasions I was transported to the bus with Jeff, the bedroom pregnant with crowing rowdies and mute nomads. I kept a flaky and yellowed lily pressed between the pages of my choir's hymnal. And yet, if there was any bitterness that crouched in the shadows waiting to gnash at my throat, the waters of Jordan that spilled down my chin and neck kept the bile quenched and quiet. I gently gathered up my son in the crook of my arm and wondered not about how I could manage life with him, but how I'd managed to live forty years without him. He was now my home and I was his.

One early morning when I was five, I had knelt on a beach facing the mighty Pacific. With my palms pressed together, I had prayed to the Lord. What was I praying for? What was in my heart? What voice had answered me? The same One Who calls me by the lightning, by the thunder, by the trumpet sound within my soul.

I reached up toward the light switch and closed down the day.

And I've learned
That we must look inside our hearts

To find a world full of love
Like yours . . . Like me . . . Like home . . . .

Lisa and Jonathan
Spring 2009

Visions of In Loveness are passed on from generation to generation.

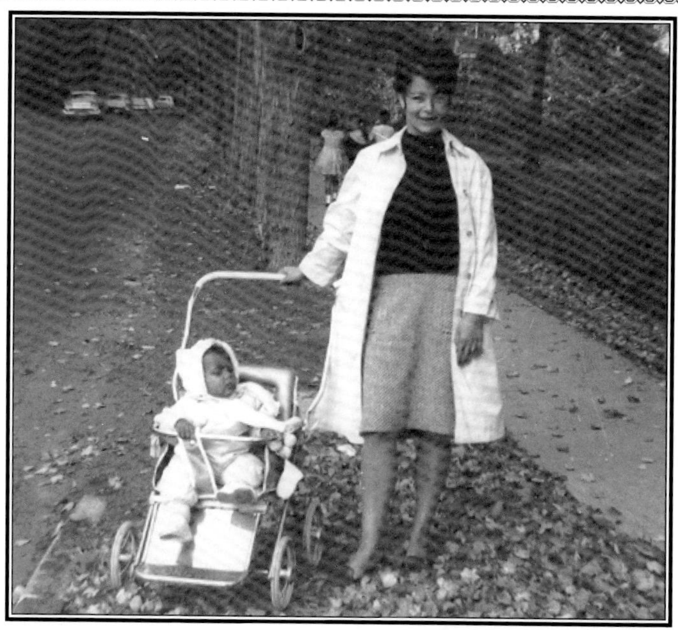

Lisa & Mother, fashion model Barbara Trent
Autumn 1965

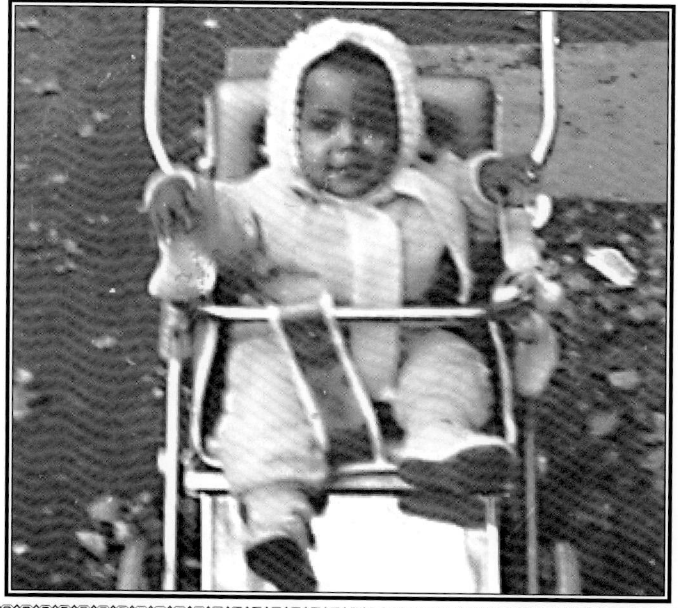

In Search of Significance

Planted within Purpose
where God's Spirit abounds
lives Christ's Significance
in His silence of sounds

God, give course to my heart
Clearly mark out my way
I'm ready to launch out
past shallow in faith's bay

Guide my mind's processing
of faith's relentless quest
Inspire in the process
my Significance's best

I'm Movin' On

"I'm sorry you didn't get drafted by one of the pro teams in the east, Willie. St. Louis is reputed to be the worst for us." Brad Pye, Jr., Sports Editor of *The Los Angeles Sentinel*, cautioned me over a meal before my departure for the Hawks training camp. There were only eight professional teams in the NBA for the upcoming 1956-57 season. I would be competing for one of eighty positions as each team's roster was limited to ten players.

"I'll be OK, Brad. Basketball has rules that can only be deviated from so far before the game will lose its integrity. The cream is rising to the top of college ball more and more each year. Fans can only be duped for so long. Talent, playing within the rules of engagement in integrated competition, has opened up unlimited possibilities. My mother continues to remind me, 'Prayer changes things.' That includes conditions in the NBA."

"Yeah, Willie. I hear you now and I heard you preach that sermon before at your final UCLA banquet. It sounds good, but it still would have been better for you if you had been drafted by New York, Philadelphia or Boston."

"I appreciate your concern, but I remind you of the summation of my departing words to the athletic department, coaches, student-athletes, families, fans and friends of UCLA Basketball: 'My mother taught me that as long as I am co-pilot for God, He knows where He wants to take me. His angels are around that course to protect me so I need not be afraid or live in fear.' Thank you again for your concern and all the encouragement your words have given me during college."

* * *

Mom, Dad, and Janice, my fiancée, waved a final goodbye through the passenger terminal windows. I ascended the steps of a TWA turbo-prop direct flight, destination St. Louis, Missouri. While adjusting my seat's position and belt, I pondered, *No Coach Wooden, no Ducky Drake to take care of the many business details and schedules of appointment times and destinations. I am on my own.* A smile came to knock down the hint of fear. Experience and training spoke forth: *Check with your Pilot first. Remember what UCLA's people did to accomplish their purpose. They were great examples and taught how to best take care of yourself when you were a student athlete. You can now take this opportunity to do it better for yourself.*

A delicious meal consumed the first hour and a half of our flight. Not until the thump of the tires touching down at St. Louis International Airport did I awaken from the peace I embraced. Thoughts about our trainer, Ducky, surfaced again. He had always taken responsibility for the baggage claim and made sure all of the team luggage and equipment was accounted for and transported to our hotel location. I rotated on my right hip to more conveniently search my front pants pocket for the claim tickets. Yep! They were there. My professional basketball career had officially begun.

I descended the portable stairs behind other passengers and entered the terminal filled with strangers, then followed the "Baggage Claim" signs and waited. Not one of the all-White passengers or personnel at either airport spoke to me or looked into my eyes, but ricocheted glances sought to promote a mindset of invisibility.

"Willie Naulls!"

"How are you, Mr. Kerner?"

His handshake had not firmed since our last

meeting in Los Angeles where we negotiated and I signed my first NBA contract. Thoughts fixed on his hesitant stare. Had he ever done an honest day's labor in his life? Could he be trusted?

"I got a rental car. You can drive us up to training camp in Galesburg, Illinois."

"That will work if that's your plan." Fortunately I had slept on the plane. Galesburg was in another state. Where was Ducky to get us a bus and driver? The reality was setting, firming up. *I am a pro, on my own now.*

The drive to camp tested my stamina and tolerance. Ben Kerner was the marquee model of the nagging back-seat driver. I was an ideal captive audience to his lecture about conditions in the South. "I'm taking a chance on you, Willie, just like the Dodgers did with Jackie Robinson. You must be aware at all times that the South is different from LA. You have to stay in self control. People here in St. Louis and in this area might call you names, but I'm sure you've been called them before." He stared my way, searching for a reaction. When he became uncomfortable with my non-response to his continuous babbling, he questioned, "Any thoughts to share with me, Willie?"

"No, Mr. Kerner. I've been hated by White folk all my life. I sensed at the airport that spirit is stronger here than in California. I was trained up by my parents to not expect much from White people as it relates to fair play and justice. We will do better when character, not color, is used as fuel for change."

There was a rattle in his throat as he recoiled to wedge himself where the seat and door met. His puzzled look filled my peripheral vision. I imagined his thoughts in silence: *"What the . . . he say?"*

After two hours of driving, my eyes dimmed as the circulation in my legs challenged to flow. "How far did you say camp was from St. Louis?"

"It's about two to two hundred fifty miles. We'll be there soon."

The first sign we passed with hope on it read "Galesburg 97 miles."

"I need something to eat and drink. Have any recommendations?"

"Pull over at the next diner. I'll get us something to go. You stay in the car. If you have to take a leak, you'll have to do it on the side of the road." He hesitated, gestured with his hands upward. "I didn't make the rules, but we will all be better off if you'll adjust your thinking to live by them."

We rolled up in front of a small three-story hotel, in name only, two hours later. In the small lobby, Mr. Kerner gestured, "Wait here by the door." He went to the desk, came back and gave me a key to a second floor room overlooking the front entrance. My roommate was a college teammate, Morrie Taft, who had arrived in camp earlier that day.

"Hey, Morrie, what's going on with this town?"

"I don't know. Just got here myself. I'm hungry. The other guys in camp just went down to a restaurant a half block from here. You want to go?"

"Sure. Could use some food."

Two other rookies, Norm Stewart and Irv Bemoras, walked with us into the small, dimly lit restaurant, found a table and sat down. All eyes focused on us. Some other players nodded to acknowledge our presence.

After about five minutes, a nervous young waitress walked over. She hesitated, flushed and opened her palms in a gesture to explain, "We don't serve niggers in here."

Three men were poised behind the counter – two with a hand underneath and in a position I thought ready for our negative reaction.

Morrie blurted out, "I don't think any nigger would want to eat in here."

We four arose and walked back to the hotel in silence. Morrie looked at me with a sarcastic "Woo-wee, Willie Naulls. We never had to deal with this kind of stuff in California."

I searched the faces of the Missouri and Illinois University grads. Nothing like empathy emerged. Ten minutes later, from the window I could see those same two players who had left with us on their way back through the restaurant's front entrance.

The telephone rang. "This is Coach Red Holzman. I understand you two were just refused service. I'm sorry about that. Can I order you some food and bring it up to you? Who is this I'm speaking to?"

"I'm Willie Naulls."

"Oh! Hi, Willie. Sorry about these people. What would you like to eat?"

This was my first experience of hostile rejection of my skin color by a retail establishment. I thought, *This has been a full first day in the NBA.* I considered going home to enjoy college and graduate school. Brad Pye's words resurfaced. A voice stammered, *Welcome, Willie Naulls.*

* * *

The next two weeks' schedule included intra-squad games in southern Missouri and Tennessee before pioneering the exposure of NBA basketball in Mexico City.

Of the fifteen players invited to training camp, my man Morrie was the last to be cut, paring the number down to twelve to finish the exhibition season. He was devastated. I considered him the most talented guard. Alone in my room now, his release alerted me to reality. Nobody in this organization cared whether I succeeded but only looked for a reason to give failing marks to my effort and, as subjectively, my attitude.

The New Hawk: Rookie Willie Naulls was ready to soar like an eagle. Abruptly – they cut his developing southern wings and sent him on an east-bound flight to the Big Apple's Nest, New York Knicks

"I know it's been only a few weeks, but you've been our best scorer, rebounder and team player,

Willie. Keep up the good work. If I may give you a word of advice, try to get along with your teammates better. They say you're a loner." Coach Red spoke sincere words and watched intently for a response.

I paused, cleared my throat. "Thank you, Coach, for your evaluation of my progress. As it relates to being a loner, you just said I play very well with the guys on the court. Off the court, away from the arena, everything is segregated. Nobody has invited me to their homes. When the game or practice is over, we go in separate directions. Why don't you set up a meeting with those of my teammates who call me a loner. Maybe they can expand on that assessment of whom they perceived me to be."

Coach Red scratched a flake off his pealing nose and shifted his weight in the chair across from where I sat in the restaurant of the recently integrated Durant Hotel in St. Louis. "We expect great things from you, Willie, including tolerating some of your teammates' discomfort. Most have never been on a team with coloreds. I know you might think we're asking a lot of you, but we've come a long way by drafting you in the first round, after all the maneuvering to get you here."

"The Hawks are paying me to play basketball and I will continue to do my best. The veterans – Coleman, Share, Pettit, Macauley and Hagan – are all seasoned pros and have made positive comments similar to yours. I believe we can win a lot of games but I admit that I have only seen two other teams play. I don't play to win a popularity contest with teammates or anyone else. I play for playing time and to win. They don't have to like me or associate with me off the court. I know and you know I have earned their respect on the court. I don't need anything else from them, just respect."

Red squirmed to relieve his discomfort. "I

appreciate your position and just wanted you to know mine." He got up and walked out the door without another word.

The telephone rang the moment I entered my room on the third floor. "Willie Naulls?"

"Yes, this is he."

"My name is Sam Wheeler. I live here in St. Louis. Welcome to our city. I'm a former Globetrotter and know how lonely it can be for a colored man his first time to a place. Are you available to go out to a club with my wife and me?

"That's a very kind offer, Sam. I'll have to check our team schedule and call you back, if that won't be an inconvenience."

"Sure, Willie. What time will you call me? It's a little after one now."

"In an hour I should have cleared my schedule with the Hawks. Thank you again for the call."

Sam and his beautiful wife picked me up that evening and drove to The Bird Cage. The featured attraction was Ike Turner. Before I could settle in my seat . . .

"Let's give a big St. Louis welcome to the new Hawk in town, Willie Naulls. Come on up here, Willie."

I made my way through the noisy overflow crowd. My knees buckled as Ike said, "We want you to know that we don't have any other colored players on any pro teams here in our town, so you're it. If anybody in here, or any colored in this town, can do anything for you, let us know. OK, Willie?"

"Thank you, Ike." Before I could say another word, a beautiful woman was on the stage, arms wrapped around my body.

"I told you, Willie. Anything we can do!"

The crowd roared. Ike went backstage as I made my way back to Sam's table. Two strangers approached me.

"Hey, Willie Naulls. Welcome to the Big Leagues."

"Thank you, man."

Sam walked between them. "This is Hank Aaron and Wes Covington. They're in town from Milwaukee."

"I follow pro baseball. It's my favorite sport." We all sat down to get better acquainted.

The stage was empty, yet guitar music filled the room from all sides. Heightened anticipation accompanied every beat. This was my first experience in a nightclub. There was an astonishing rhythmic undercurrent vibrating roar that energized my soul.

Ike's band appeared from behind a curtain. A beautiful woman friend of the Wheelers asked, "Willie Naulls, can men from California dance?"

"I don't know about all the men out there, but this one wants you to teach me."

She smiled, extended her hand, and I was out of my seat, caught up in the beat. Hank, Wes and Sam were doing a dance I had never seen. Everyone was so engaged in Ike's music they didn't even notice my learning curve. This new sensation my emotions had never experienced.

Back at the hotel, the flashing lights still pulsed to the beat of the band as I attempted to turn the volume off in my mind. *These people here in St. Louis sure are nice to me* closed down my conscious thoughts at three in the morning.

The Hawks' first home game at Kiel Auditorium was a sellout. When I was announced as a starting guard, the roar of the crowd was encouraging. A poll conducted by the local *St. Louis Post Dispatch* to determine the most popular player voted Willie Naulls to be that Soaring Hawk. Some veterans were more visibly challenged than others, but all of my teammates were insecure due to my confidence and pride in my heritage.

In an interesting development, one player on the team called me to talk about race relations in the South. Jack Coleman, a veteran of many teams, said to me one evening. "Willie, I want to apologize for the attitudes of the White people here in the South. The restaurant is segregated and I believe that's the reason you're not invited. You can use my car if you'd like."

"What restaurant, Jack?"

"You mean no one even told you about the team banquet tonight at Stan Musial's restaurant? I'm sorry, Willie."

I didn't know what to say. "Thanks for calling, Jack, and for offering your car."

Fifteen minutes later Dr. Stan London, team physician, called. "Willie, I heard they didn't invite you to the banquet tonight. I called to tell you how sorry I am for the humiliation you must feel. Is there anything I can do for you?"

"No. Thank you, Dr. London, for calling."

I hung up in the silence of my own thoughts. Owner Ben Kerner had warned me of the insensitive racism in the South, but he forgot to include his part. Apparently "The South's" attitude extended as far north as throughout St. Louis, Missouri, and Galesburg, Illinois.

It wasn't long before Kerner walked up to me as I dressed after practice. "I've traded you to New York for guard Slater Martin. You are to report immediately. See Marty for the details."

There was a hush as I strolled across the court and out the door. Jack Coleman shouted, "Wait up, Willie!" I turned to receive his extended hand. "I'm sorry to see you go, but you'll be respected more in

New York. You're a great guy and a great talent. Don't let these yo-yos discourage you."

"Thank you, Jack, and I wish you the best too."

Marty Blake, Kerner's all-purpose man, intercepted my course. "Willie, here's an airplane ticket for tomorrow morning, two days' meal money (twelve dollars) and some cab fare to the airport. Once you land in New York, you're their responsibility." He turned without another word and slew footed back up the stairs.

It took me a few hours to say goodbye to my landlord and her family, and to some other fine people I had met in St. Louis. The next morning I arose early to meet the taxi I had scheduled to drive me to the airport. There was a chill in the air. Mrs. Cook drew near, wrapping her arms around me inside my overcoat.

"Willie, I pray you won't think badly of all of us here in St. Louis. We loved having you here. It doesn't seem fair because the people appreciate you and want you on the team." Her grip lessened as she stepped backward to look up into my eyes.

I smiled in response. "Thank you. I will never forget your kindness."

Mrs. Cook, a woman in her fifties, lost her temporarily elevated social status in the Black community that day. She had been host to the first and only athlete of color on an integrated professional team in that area.

I waved goodbye to a few neighbors who readied for the work day. The cab driver asked, "What airline, sir?"

"TWA, please." The trip to the airport was short and uneventful. Traffic was not a problem, small town light compared to LA.

During the ride, there was not enough time to collect and organize my thoughts about my St. Louis experience. What came to mind was the first overnight train ride to Chicago after a game. The accommodations were excellent, a private sleeper berth. Through the oversized window, I saw rural countryside and small towns before entering into the sprawling influence of Chicago. The walk from the train to the taxi area was the coldest experience of my life. We boarded Braniff Airlines that morning for a game in Minneapolis against the Lakers. Wow, what an experience.

The second thought was a trip to Indiana. The plane landed in a blizzard. The players assembled in a very small, under-heated terminal and waited two hours for a bus to pick us up to drive the fifty miles to Fort Wayne, home of the Zollner Pistons. I met Joe Jackson and his developing family of entertainers after a night club performance that night in Fort Wayne. They were sensational. His famous son Michael would be born two years later. The Pistons franchise moved to Detroit soon thereafter. We players were pioneers of an experiment. Obviously it has worked.

The overcast weather obscured the scene of New York's skyline I had viewed from the airplane upon arrival the year before when UCLA had come to play in the Holiday Festival. The cab ride from LaGuardia Airport to Time Square's Paramount Hotel introduced the difference between "down on the plantation" and "bright lights – big city." My new temporary address was 46th Street between 8th and Broadway. The new workplace was three blocks north on 8th Avenue at 49th Street, Madison Square Garden.

I was hesitant to get excited but everywhere tempted. "Hey, Will. Welcome to New York." That greeting continued from the airport through my first season.

The cab driver gave me an analysis of the Knicks roster. "McGuire, Braun, Gallatin and 'Sweets' Clifton are getting old. We welcome some young blood on the team. I saw you when you came to town with UCLA. You'll help the Knicks. They need you."

It was juice for my soul to not have the racial issue overbearing. The experience was similar to moving from Dallas to Los Angeles when I was nine years old. Every person who said "Welcome" was covered with White skin. What a difference a day made. The porter who took the bags to escort me to a room said, "Welcome to New York, Mr. Naulls. Good luck with the Knicks. There are a variety of options that you have for entertainment and dining within a few blocks. If we can be of any service to you, please call."

"Thank you."

The room was small but adequate. And, God had delivered me out of the Hawks' cotton patch, into the Big Apple, to experience the next phase of His opportunities to be blessed and to glorify Him.

Looking at Me through Your Eyes

Looking at me through your eyes
raises the question on which doubt thrives
Can I ever know without a shadow of doubt
that you really do care what I am all about?
Skin to skin – White looking – Black back at you
Did you ever want to know me, a friendship to
pursue?
. . . .

A Stutter – at the Brink of Change
The Starting Five

Professional basketball took up ten years of my life in playing time and ten years of amateur preparation to get there. In spite of what some have labeled "the dark days" of race relations in the NBA, African-American players used the experiences as growth platforms. Every racial intrusion served as a strengthening exercise for the next encounter.

One of those growth exercises occurred during a game at Madison Square Garden. New York Knicks Coach Fuzzy Levane, a challenged stutterer, lost his temper and was ejected for cursing at a referee. Teams didn't hire assistant coaches. The NBA's m.o. at that time was for a coach removed for conduct deemed inappropriate to designate the team captain as his replacement, and Fuzzy had selected me for that game. (Later, under Carl Braun, when my teammates voted me to be Captain, I became the first African-American elected captain of any integrated professional sports team.) The sold-out crowd watched the unfolding drama with bated breath.

Fuzzy, exasperated, walked toward our team huddled in front of the bench, looked back over his shoulder and barked, "Y–You're missing a g–g–good game, you blind . . . ." He then pushed through my teammates with extended arms, put both hands on my shoulders, looked into my eyes and, in his moment of rage, stuttered, "Wil– Wil– Wil–lie, you ta–a–ke . . . ." His eyes widened. He looked down to my skin color, then back, and back again to my skin. "Uh, ju – just a – a – a min – minute, Wil – Wil-lie . . . . Willie, I – I – I'm so – so – sor – rry!" He looked past me, walked over to our trainer, whispered something in his ear, soberly walked back onto the court to a referee, whispered to him. As though orchestrating by pressure to conform to the current racial norm, he calmly strolled to the scorers' table at mid-court and relayed his decision. The crowd roared its approval of his tirade and applauded as he waved a smile as he exited toward the locker room.

New York Knicks
1958-59
Standing:
Trainer Don Friederichs • Willie Naulls • Mike Farmer
Ray Felix • Charlie Tyra • Kenny Sears • Pete Brennan
Seated:
Ron Sobie • Frank Selvy • Coach Fuzzy Levane
Carl Braun • Richie Guerin • Jack George

In the spirit of unspoken and united white-skinned bureaucratic collaboration, the announcer obediently informed the crowd that our trainer, Don Fredericks, would take over the coaching duties of the Knicks. "Fuzzy has told me to take over on the bench, and . . . uh . . . you, Willie, you're still our Captain and leader on the court." Donnie looked like the principle of Peter – overwhelmed. A question of who stutter-stepped whom arose in my mind as it fought to keep rage harnessed.

What an historic precedent could have been quietly set, without fanfare, that night. Bill Russell would become the first full-time African-American coach in the NBA some eight years later. Destiny unfolds God's plan, experience upon experience.

I am certainly not the only player to have been a victim in such situations, to have a groove carved in my memory resulting in an inflammable keloid. It's uncomfortable, yet I don't stutter to unveil these unrecorded memories. Ten years of experience with groups of men in hot pursuit of one goal, NBA glory, don't just disappear. What a relief to my soul to regurgitate the spoils of that mean-spirited stud war. Only God could influence leaders to call right right and wrong wrong.

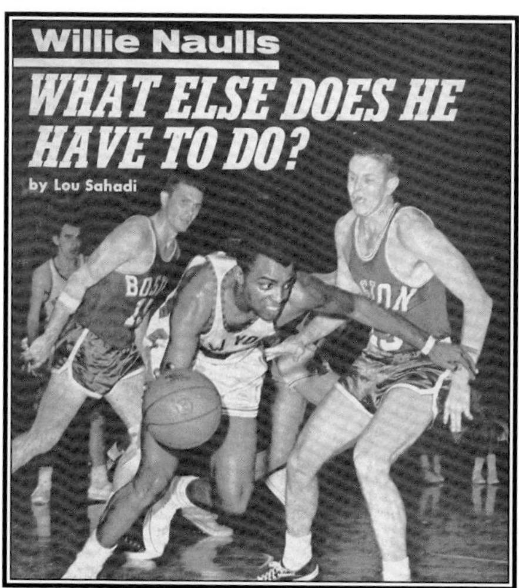
Willie Naulls

WHAT ELSE DOES HE HAVE TO DO?

by Lou Sahadi

Lou Sahadi questions how much more Willie must do to gain respect in this national sports magazine.

The point here is to lay bare the humiliating conditions under which African-American athletes endured the weight of social change. Jackie Robinson once told me, "To take any more unprovoked, abusive attacks without fighting back could harm me emotionally and spiritually. I don't promote violence in reaction to injustice and I strive to live in self control." African-American athletes pondered whether White people thought it understandable when individuals succumbed to the human instinct to fight back, especially when the stutter of a moan for peace and justice was completely ignored.

Wisdom teaches, "If it depends on you, live at peace with everyone" (Romans 12:18). I was taught, "If it is possible . . . just endure it! There is power in self control." That's what African-American parents of the ghettos taught, by example, to my generation of NBA players. Those young aspiring professionals who followed took the banner to new heights of expression. Men like Magic Johnson and Michael Jordan exceeded our dream. They were made stronger by ingesting the truth of their roots.

If every athlete of color had responded to violent attacks with retaliatory counter punches, the possibility of unjust judgment and punishment would have increased. Martin Luther King, Jr., emphasized that everyone has the capacity for self-control, to promote peace and justice. Victory comes when athletes as role models for youth resist the temptation to be ensnared in a trap. Inside the open cage, bait is placed for rage to rush into the trap of mean-spirited people.

"Don't be overcome by evil, but overcome evil with good." Mom's voice was clear. That word is the Spirit of Stutter, God's Word, to remind us that He is the Lamp unto our feet and the Light unto our path.

* * *

Another growth spurt began as I rode from the

airport through the streets of downtown Boston in Hall of Famer Bill Russell's new play toy – a Lincoln Continental convertible. "I have all the latest options." His eyes beamed obsession. "This is the finest automobile ever made. Look at this." He pressed a button and the solid roof recoiled into the trunk.

With happiness in his face and a cackle in his voice he laughed out of control. "My my my, Westwood Willie, I'm so glad I enticed you to come out of retirement to play with the Celtics. We'll make you a champion before you retire again." A week later he got a bigger laugh at the sight of me throwing up during the first day of Coach Auerbach's grueling training camp.

We have never discussed it in depth, but Russ, Tom Sanders, Sam Jones, K.C. Jones and I emerged that year to comprise the first all-African-American starting team in the history of integrated professional sports. Coach's decision was historic and altered the NBA's course. Because we won World Championships each of my three years on the team, public opinion about race relations in sports rotated on its axis. Coach Red Auerbach's historic decision to start five black-skinned men had a simple purpose. We were the best combination of talent he had to put on the court – to win. What has been ignored is that it opened the door for unrestrained competition to seek its highest level of expression.

"**The Starting Five**," immortalized on canvas by artist Ernie Barnes, has never been given its proper place in the history of the NBA. From zero African-American players on any NBA team prior to 1950 to five starters on the NBA Championship team in the 1963-64 season: That's a black skin coup, which only God foreknew, and orchestrated too. To Him be the glory.

Hope

When Hope is tarred and feathered
and God's Will is kept on hold
there standing at its guard gate
is a death wish on that soul

One's will to desire freely
with some confidence – is Hope
The substance of heart's direction
releases one's faith to cope

Hope is good medication
smiling through your Faith to cure
Every sprung up weed doubt plants
is hewn for Christ to mature

Who's Got Your Back?

Peggy was not surprised by discomfort in her back. Doctors had advised over the years of a genetic predisposition for disc related weakness. Two years previously, at age 36, she had suffered a ruptured disc, requiring surgery for the first time. She feared the worst when a month long series of muscular spasms cautioned her to restrict activities. "I am fearful to make any sudden movement," she lamented to friends.

As she pondered her fate, children played in full view through the front window of their home in Port Naches, Texas. An urge to sneeze without restraint overcame her. Ah-choo! Like a lightning bolt, pain paralyzed. To her knees, she crumpled to the floor. Her immediate thought: I can't breathe without pain. It's impossible to move.

"Phil! Help me, Phil," she cried out. "It's my back."

The pain was unbearable. Her husband helped her from the living room floor down the hall to the master bedroom. Peggy and Phil had been high school sweethearts and had married six months after their graduation. He had always been her rock in times of need. "What medication do we have? I'll call the doctor," Phil offered. "Be calm, honey. Let's pray for God's intervention."

Peggy had been confirmed and baptized as a Christian at the age of twelve in her family's church, but didn't know the Lord spiritually. Phil had been raised in a family of strong faith, and because she fell in love, she opted to join his church's youth activities during high school. She attended church regularly once they were married, but believes her true salvation came on a night while watching Billy Graham on television. Because of that born-again experience, Peggy was confident to pray in faith for healing. She trusted in God.

A call to her orthopedic surgeon revealed that he was out of town, but the good news was that he was scheduled to arrive back that day and return to the office the next. The bad news: "If you need surgery, his schedule is completely booked for the week," the office manager cautioned.

Peggy contacted her prayer group. "Please be in agreement with our prayers that the doctor's schedule will be relieved to accommodate my needs."

Pain pills didn't help. Peggy spent most of the night standing. There was no comfort to be found lying in bed. She thought about little else but relief of the agony.

The two hour drive to Houston was dreadful. Phil brought pillows to help Peggy position herself comfortably in the back seat, but the pain intensified by the minute. She believed the Lord was with her every mile of the way. When the pain got worse with every turn of the car, every bump in the highway, she prayed for God's intervention. "Jesus, it hurts so bad. Please, Lord, I don't want to think that the doctor can't see me. Help me, Lord."

The nurse welcomed Peggy with news. "Good morning. A new medical procedure called magnetic resonance imaging – MRI – is available. We can schedule it for tomorrow. You'll be flat on your back and rolled into a space just big enough for you to fit. It'll be like your whole body is inside a big pipe. You're not claustrophobic, are you?"

"Yes, I am. I fear closed spaces. I always have."

"Well, you decide." The nurse shrugged her shoulders but fixed her eyes in a sincere appeal. "The

MRI is supposed to give more information than an x-ray. The doctor can better pinpoint exactly where and what your problem is."

Peggy and Phil spent that night with her younger sister, Cindy, in Katy but again was unable to find a comfortable position and slept little. By morning she was barely able to walk but determined to try the new MRI. She relied on Phil and Cindy to help her into and out of the car.

The traffic crunch fueled Peggy's mental and physical trauma, but when she entered the door of the radiology office and saw the technicians' empathic smiles, she was relieved. Her tolerance of pain gladly received the undergirding. The thought of knowing exactly what was wrong inspired hope in each dreaded step.

The technician helped her into the device, repeating earlier instructions emphatically, "Don't move!" Peggy didn't see how that would be possible. The apparatus was just big enough to squeeze her body inside the circular pipe-like space.

As she prayerfully entered into the MRI device, a zone of her worst fear, she softly personalized God's Word of Truth: "God will keep in perfect peace her whose mind is steadfast because she trusts in Him."

Immediately every pain in her body ceased. Instantly, in her mind, the device which surrounded her body was God. "You are this enclosure around me, Lord. Praise your holy name, Jesus." Peggy had never had such peace nor been more aware of God's presence than at that moment.

Halfway through the long procedure, she felt a nose itch. Again, in a soft voice, her lips moved without detection. "Help me, Lord, not to give in to this impulse. You know my every thought, my every need. I cast all my care on You, for You care for me." Miraculously she sensed her nose being scratched.

Again, she relaxed into God's peace.

Forty-five minutes later, upon leaving the MRI, the excruciating pain returned. The technician said, "The images will not be read until tomorrow." Peggy was disappointed with the delay, but had confidence that God was aware of her needs.

Later that day, the doctor's staff called to say that the MRI had been read and showed a huge rupture of a disc. Then she heard the good report. "One of the doctor's patients had to cancel her operation, so the doctor is able to do your surgery tomorrow."

Peggy and Phil praised God and thanked Him for making His presence known during the successful operation and recovery period. He confirmed that they could trust Him in any situation.

* * *

Years later, during her older sister's ordeal with ovarian cancer, Peggy awoke during an all night vigil in the hospital's waiting room. She altered her position in a chair, reached for her bag and again experienced excruciating pain. An examination revealed that scar tissue from her previous surgery had ruptured. Armed with the experience of healing through strong faith, she did what was required to manage her own health and still assisted Sheryl. In a few months she was able to resume her normal routine. Friends and family members praised God for Peggy's witness of answered prayers for healing. She became God's missionary of hope.

Her mother called one morning from the home of her ill sister in Port Naches. "We need to take Sheryl to M.D. Anderson Hospital right now!"

She left work and drove to her sister's home, praying all the way. "Lord, you know my intense fear of driving in traffic, especially in Houston. Your Word has taught me that I am more than a conqueror in Christ Jesus. I must drive in traffic, and I will not yield to fear."

Twenty minutes into the two-hour drive, her desperately ill sister pleaded, "Peggy, can't you drive faster? I need to get to the hospital. I feel like I'm dying."

Peggy prayed, "Lord, I know you parted the Red Sea, so I am confident You can part this traffic for us."

She fumbled with the controls to turn on the caution lights so other drivers would know there was an emergency. As she sped along the freeway at 80 to 85 miles per hour, she could see the cars parting as she approached. Peggy blessed every vehicle and driver she passed and arrived at the hospital a full 45 minutes faster than any other trip during that time of day.

She hurried for assistance and helped put Sheryl in a wheelchair before giving the keys to the valet. "Will you please turn off the flashers for me?"

The attendant looked confused. "Lady, the flashers aren't on."

Peggy was puzzled, then not surprised. It became obvious to her that it wasn't the flashers parting the traffic. It was God's Hand which had opened a way between the cars, just as it had been His Hand that had soothed the discomfort of her nose and His arms which had surrounded her in that tight MRI space, giving her His peace. She pondered as she sat comforting her mom, awaiting the doctors' evaluation of her sister, "God is faithful and has made Himself a living reality in my life. To Him be the glory, forever and ever, Amen!"

The Celtic Bench Is Cold

Battle lines of Black and White
had dimmed because of score
"Winning it all" year after year
exalted the Race of Blacks' poor

Covenant team changed the guard
their motto a higher call
Battle scars did supersede
racial lines to "Win it all"

. . . .

Competition Seeks Its Highest Level of Expression

Sitting on the pine was a new and not-so-pleasant experience, even on the World Champions' bench. The humiliation of being a Celtic in name only reverberated an alarm in my ego. An All-Star-caliber producer for most of my career, the last three seasons of a ten-year professional stint were similarly successful. I had always started and been an integral part of any team for which I had played since grammar school. The sense of not being considered important to the production of fame was a blow to my standard of earning my stripes.

Blindsided by trust in a roommate, in a moment of honest sharing after abruptly awakening out of a mid-afternoon slumber's dream about fierce competition, "I missed the last shot. . . ." Rubbing my eyes, I sat up on the side of the bed. Before I could finish with "of the third quarter" he vaulted on his way out the door. Eagerly, I waited in anticipation to share the rest of the dream, but he never returned. He missed the best part. We came back to win, and I made the game's winning shot. The only thing he heard was, "Uh–hey, man… I had this strange dream … we were losing … I missed the last shot … ."

The game that night was our next encounter. I walked past him to get to my locker next to Don Nelson. "Hey, Willie, what's up?" I nodded acknowledgment but fixed my eyes on my roommate. Nothing! He stared past a fixed point between his big toes and had very little to say, as did the other guys. Even "Buddy," our normally verbose trainer, was subdued as he taped my ankles for battle.

Red's voice, coarse but committed, broke the silence. "I've changed the Starting Five." With no explanation, "Hondo, you start with Satch up front. This is the most important game of the season. We gotta win!" Not a look or word in our direction. No one appeared surprised. I was numb but ready to play. To deepen what I perceived to be an insult, I was given very little time in the remaining playoff games. This was the third and last of my championship years with the Celtics.

For months afterward, selfishly, I could not shed the sense of humiliation for what I surmised to be a traumatic Auerbachism. His shutting down communication, based solely on what I assumed one veteran had reported, stunned me. Pride didn't permit me to confront him, nor my former roommate, to vent rage. Bottom line: The Celtics were only seeking their best competitive level of expression. They did what they thought was best for the team. Ostensibly, it worked. We won our ninth championship in ten years – and without this Rare Rock. At the thought, I smiled to relieve the pent up anguish in my soul. I was ready to move on.

This is the first attempt to relieve the stored up, almost forgotten, unforgiveness in my heart for these many years. There has been no apparent sense of need of explanation from anyone associated with that team. Without a word of sensitivity from any Celtic of that group about my soul's bent on the notion of a tarnished reputation, our relationships dried up as is common among professional athletes after retirement. In hindsight, very little could have been done short of direct confrontation to extinguished the smoldering desire for the truth to be told, to experience a sense of retribution. My parents had convinced me early on with their words, "You're rare, son. Grow through working out of yourself God's uniqueness of purpose for your life. Don't let the acts of men and women who don't wish you well distract you from the path God has prepared for you alone." Yeah! But . . . my ego shot back at the voices' attempt to comfort, with not common, but what Mom called good, sense.

When our paths have crossed, Red and my former teammates have been enthusiastically cordial and complimentary of my family's development since retirement. But no one has ever mentioned, nor have I broached the subject of, my roommate's and Red's negative assessment of what they perceived to be my character. That has been a tough but maturing lesson to ingest.

In retrospect, I joined the Celtics organization in awe of its winning tradition. The character of the coach or individual players was never an issue. NBA Champions, six of the seven years before I got there and the three years during my membership, was the excitement. The bottom line to the Celtics basketball tradition was winning. Thought of casualties inflicted in the process would have distracted focus. They made the right decision. To insert Hall of Famer Hondo Havlicek into the starting lineup instead of leaving him to fulfill his normal sixth-man role inspired the team to go from very good to great – and another crown.

When rejected or demoted in role play assignment, silence was the contribution expected of each player to not impede the team's rush to win, to "go all the way." From that perch, I retired at the end of my tenth season.

Bill Keane, one of the town's reputed "poison pen" reporters asked, "Willie, why aren't you starting or playing any longer?"

I responded, "No comment until the end of the playoffs."

The next day the headlines read, "Naulls to Retire at the End of this Playoff Season."

Coach Red went "code red" livid. For the first time in days he was in my face spewing his cigar juice on my practice gear. "What the hell you thinking about, Willie? You should know better than talk to these ******* reporters. You should have come to me to announce you wanna quit. I could have traded and got somethin' for ya!" The retaliatory shock on my face at his sudden attack backed him up for a stride or two for space.

It took all my energy not to scream laughter from the depths of my being. His honesty relieved all my suspicions. It was all about his image and control. At that moment my soul groaned, *It has to be all about me now.* Every player involved in sports would be stronger to have heard Red's bureaucratic truth. The stain on his teeth glistened, his eyes strained to promote guilt as the words echoed in my psyche, "You should have come to me, Willie. You should know better." Lowering his eyes to deflect my glare's resolve, he stuttered, "You should have talked to me first, Willie. You owe me that much respect."

There was an uncomfortable silence among the Celtic lambs. I stared back through their collective comfort zone. Nothing to hint of empathy for my righteous indignation. Red knew I was not one of his mental lambs. I thought, *Here's a future Hall of Famer by reputation, but who is he really? Come to him first? He hasn't spoken to me since he got a foul and distorted word from my roommate – and soul brother. He intentionally avoided talking to me man to man, face to face, to discuss his decision to bench me. I understand that in the middle of battle is not the time for family feuds to be resolved. But a direct command to a proven battle tested and seasoned warrior would be considered sound therapy in most organizations. But not Red's team. I have been respectful to not cause a scene during the playoffs. He expected his players to be mute. He should keep those reporters out of my face. Did he even consider that I never mentioned retirement? He perceived a lack of loyalty to his authority. Does he even value me as a man? Not a boy? He never asked me if I spoke to the reporter about retirement, but he just assumed.*

I looked around the locker room. Nobody looked in my eyes. Under my breath, I mumbled as my parents' voices emerged, "You are Rare. Rebuke evil reports. You are a man. Demand respect that you have earned."

"Machine Gun Tommy," one of the Hall of Fame retired Celtic greats, had advised me in private conversation during his last season, "When Red is through with a player, he forgets you were ever there. Just remember, when you are no longer thought of as a prime time producer, you had better review your options." Heiny's advice is sage counsel for professional athletes of any sport, even today.

To rally my self esteem, I uttered under my breath a conditioned reflex, "There's one thing he can't demand, even has to earn, and that is my respect for him as a man. Whether he cares for me or not is irrelevant. Ego babbling contesting the last word is trivia. It's time to move on!"

It is commonly known that most Celtic opponents hated Red, referring to him as rude, crude, selfish, condescending, egomaniacal and myopic. Didn't bother him; only made him enjoy winning more. These back-hand compliments to the not-so-benevolent dictator grew his image to legendary proportions. Envied, tolerated and forgiven, his uniqueness was glorified because his teams won year after year. His cigar-lighting victory celebration on the bench at game's end, often occurring long before the final buzzer sounded, became legendary, to the delight of the Celtic

Willie and "Hondo" Havlicek cheer as game's end is near, evidenced by Red's victory cigar

faithful. Coach Red influenced players' futures after retirement, as several succeeded Russell, the first African-American to coach in the NBA. I never contemplated alternatives in pro basketball. Any athlete will tell you, a coach has power to manipulate his future. In the process, Celtic players did respect the coach's right and authority to be the leader he chose to be. I agreed wholeheartedly, as that was the precise mission of the civil rights movement of that time. People were dying as we waged our ego battles in the trenches of pro sports' integration forefront.

Was our war relevant to the overall struggle for each person's right to be "me, myself and I"? I know with every breath of life given me that individualism was the driving force that fueled my hope.

Professional basketball is a game to non-participants, but to players it is a business in which uniquely talented individuals compete for team supremacy. The law of supply and demand is in full effect. The question for every participant to ponder: When an owner evaluates a player to be expendable to his organization, what should the athlete's mindset be? My suggestion? Objectively review options. Control the experience. Make a plan for the future in advance. Don't let negative experiences seethe inside to act as a canker worm eating away to erode personal and team progress. Meet with the coach and owners and be prepared to ask specific questions. To work out the full measure of one's created purpose is a life long endeavor.

The New York Knicks had prepared me well for the business insensitivity of management toward players. An incident in the prime of my pro career is a case in point. All-Star NBA athletes, representing their teams, were solicited and paid for appearances at youth summer camps in upstate New York and Pennsylvania. The Knicks contacted me via telephone in California. I agreed conditionally to participate. The terms were very clear. "Mr. Podesta, you know I have been the four-time All-Star and Captain of the Knicks. You will have to pay me a fee equal to the highest paid to any other participant."

The General Manager of the Knicks cleared his throat to let a pregnant time pass in his pause – a typical negotiating ploy, I thought.

"OK, Willie, we'll treat you fair." We ended on an optimistic note. "We're honored to have you represent the Knicks."

I arrived back in New York a month later to learn from another All-Star player and teammate that his fee was higher than what the GM had committed for my participation. "Thank you for the insight, Richie. Your honesty is appreciated. I'll not reveal you as the source of truth."

"OK, Willie. I don't want to be put in the middle. They told me to keep it confidential, not tell anyone. But I thought you should know."

"I won't forget your trust and kindness."

The next day, I called the Knicks owner. "You have breached our verbal agreement. I will not participate in the camps." There was silence as I hung up, after refusing to reveal the source of my information.

Promoters had already begun to use my name and image to advertise their summer sports camps' activities in New York's major publications. The Knicks management went into orbit proclaiming to the media, "Willie Naulls does not honor his word. Willie Naulls is a ball player who breaks contracts." The headlines were filled with Naulls' character assassination.

I defended my decision during an interview with a reporter for *The New York Post*. "The content of my agreement with the Knicks, a verbal agreement with the GM, will prove your reporting to be based on incomplete research. Here is a copy of the letter confirming my agreement with them. They violated that agreement." I continued, "My witness is the team's secretary. The Knicks organization wrote me this letter of confirmation at my request." The Knicks and *The Post* were shocked to know that I had a written schedule of dates and terms on Knicks stationery, sent to me in California before I left Los Angeles to come to New York. "Don't you trust us, Willie?" Ned Irish, the owner, gestured in an attempt at humor. The GM, on vacation in Florida, was reportedly stunned to learn that his secretary and I had confirmed the facts of the telephonic agreement in writing.

In a full retraction, the Knicks acquiesced, apologized and paid me the top compensation plus a bonus to buy their own relief. I learned from experience that it was truly a negotiating war between management and players. There are times when a player has the advantage. For example: LeBron James, 2009 MVP, in the last year of his contract with Cleveland, before free agency. Now that's a real power position from which to negotiate.

Russ was the one man who could have risen up publicly to slap some of that cigar spit down the coach's throat. He did, through selling an example of an effective way to deal with authority. It was simple and practical. Never publicly confront the spirit of selfish pride of a coach. Do everything within your capacity to win championships. Handle personal grievances privately with the coach. In Coach Auerbach's time of glory, the Celtics won the NBA Championship nine of eleven years. Russ won eleven out of thirteen years, nine as a player, then twice during the three years he was player/coach. His great reward for not confronting but respecting authority openly has been life-long opportunity to graciously reap the benefits and honor of his *earned* international reputation of being the greatest athlete of all time. With emphasis, I repeat: with two NCAA Championships, an Olympic Gold Medal, and eleven NBA Championship rings, he is the greatest athlete who ever competed in the history of basketball.

Sitting through that final 1965-66 Championship banquet was interesting. Our hero shed tears and Coach Red and my roommate and family privately shared their cheers; but no one acknowledged the end of my pro basketball years. Not a word. I had violated Red's code.

In hindsight, my rebellion in silence and reputed unauthorized announcement of retirement hadn't demonstrated Red's expected standard of loyal and obedient behavior. After all was said and done, we were World Champs again. Bill Russell, Tom Sanders, K.C. Jones, Sam Jones and I had comprised the first all-Black-skinned Starting Five in the history of integrated professional sports. But, to our team's unrecorded credit, skin color had second billing – or no billing – to the winning tradition's loyalty. And that attitude proved to be right. The truth was marching on and no one even recognized the progress. A Black skinned player proved his loyalty to integration's theme and innocently gave false testimony about another Black skinned player, tainting my pre-game dream, and it was done in the spirit of what's best for the team." It is of less importance that he was wrong. The end and most important result in professional sports was (and is) winning, and not the character tainting of its gladiators. I reiterate. Although my roommate was wrong in his blind and insensitive rush to judgment, he was clearly demonstrating what he believed to be expected behavior in Celtic ranks, loyalty to Coach Red and his legacy. The team's core value of "just win, baby" had been established before I got there. Celtic players, including this author, were servants to the winning tradition and routinely sacrificed individual plights. Winning at all costs, regardless of human casualties, was and is the most honored goal to promote fame and fortune. Of course I survived, a stronger person, with an advancing and better prepared defense to withstand the many onslaughts to follow.

Legends like the Celtics of my era have reputations of greatness of performance during a measure of time. I have been honored in some circles as one, but less than that to others through which I have come. The intent herein is to rid myself of any unforgiveness hidden in the recesses of my heart. Earnest reporting brings truth into light. Purging my soul, seeking truth and forgiving are noble goals, which I promote. My parents' words stalked and emerged when I thought the spiritual boot of discrimination and disrespect was resting heavily upon the nape of my neck: "William, make the Lord your Rock and Fortress and Deliverer. We have prayed that He would give you opportunities based on your talent and preparation." I needed to realize that the Spirit of competition was seeking its highest level of expression.

I am rare, only because I have long abided in the Rock, Jesus Christ, the Righteous. I am more than a conqueror through Him who loves me. If God is for me, who can be against me? I was one of those who had ushered in the era of merit-based promotion in sports. So when the light dimmed in the twilight of my career, I had to step aside and let the next star rise and shine.

1965 - 66 WORLD CHAMPION BOSTON CELTICS

Standing, left to right: Ron Bonham, Don Nelson, Tom Sanders, Mel Counts, John Thompson, Woody Sauldsberry, Willie Naulls, Sam Jones, Larry Siegfried, Trainer Buddy LeRoux
Sitting, left to right: John Havlicek, K. C. Jones, Chairman of the Board Marvin Kratter, Coach Red Auerbach, President John J. Waldron, Bill Russell

Willie and His Hall of Fame NBA Teammates

Player	PPG	RPG	Proficiency
Wilt Chamberlain	30.07	22.89	37.92
Bill Russell	15.08	22.45	29.99
Bob Pettit	26.36	16.22	29.40
Tom Heinsohn	18.64	8.79	18.11
Clyde Lovellette	16.97	9.46	17.94
Willie Naulls	15.79	9.09	16.98
John Havlicek	20.78	6.30	16.69
Harry Gallatin	12.97	9.80	16.28
Edward Macauley	17.52	6.75	15.51
Cliff Hagan	17.72	6.62	15.48
Sam Jones	17.69	4.94	13.78
Frank Ramsey	13.45	5.47	12.20
Tom Satch Sanders	9.57	6.33	11.12
K. C. Jones	7.41	3.55	7.26
Red Holzman	6.05	0.96	3.98

PPG = career points per game   RPG = career rebounds per game
Proficiency = Career PPG/2 + Career RPG

Willie's Hall of Fame NBA Coaches

Coach	Total Games	Games Won	Percentage
Red Auerbach	1,417	938	66.2 %
Red Holzman	1,300	696	53.5 %

From the alley of his birth called Jutson Court in Dallas, to World Championships in professional basketball in Boston, to real estate development in the community of his youth in Watts, God has been there to accomplish great things in the life of author Willie Naulls

Willie Naulls
Three-time World Champion
Boston Celtics

Opening Day
Willie Naulls Shopping Plaza
Watts, California

Friendship

Friendship . . .
is like mining for gold
rare to unearth
rare to unfold

. . . .

A Second Chance

"What time will you pick me up?" I asked with slightly over-the-top enthusiasm. Carla was a girl I'd met in the church choir. Really one of the few people I felt I related to—confident, kind of hip and quirky, not really interested in anything generic or status quo. Cool AND Christian? Didn't think it was possible.

"I'll be at your place at around nine, nine thirty. "

Nine thirty?! I thought. We wouldn't be getting to the Valley 'til ten. A little late to get started. Ten was usually when I thought about heading home from a night out. But these were Carla's people, her circle. She was nice enough to invite me in to the fold.

"That's cool. Should we caravan?"

"No, I'll drive" she answered with a certainty I admired.

* * *

Three weeks prior we sat next to each other in choir. I'd sung with the group for a while and she was the newbie. With each anthem we rehearsed, she seemed to lean in a little closer to me, trying to get the "goods" on what type of voice I had. Was I pretty good for an amateur, just fa la la filler, or was I a serious contender? Carla was on her way to being a real pro. She'd already made a demo and sang pretty regularly at local clubs.

"I'm just singing in this choir because I love God and I love the music. In the natural, my professional career is really starting to take off. The folks here feel like family though and are always willing to give a hand." And winking, she hid both of us from the director with her music and whispered, "See that cute tenor over there? He gave me greater hand last week."

She was definitely like no other Christian I'd ever met. She continued, taking advantage of the director's momentary focus on the tenors. "I really wish there were a way to merge my career with love of worshiping Jesus through song. There's just not a lot of money in Christian music."

I didn't really feel like debating with her. Amy Grant and the Gaithers would probably beg to differ. I wanted to tell her not to worry about the money and follow her heart, but somehow, the only thing that managed to clumsily slip out of my mouth was "Totally."

My phone rang at about 5:00am. Man oh man, I thought, somebody better be dead or having a heart attack or something. Suddenly Fred Sanford appeared before my eyes, gripping his chest and pronouncing his famous "I'm comin' to see you, Elizabeth." Not nice, Lis. I wonder what Jesus would have to say about all this. "Hello?!"

"Oh, hi, uh, Lisa. It's Lisa, right?"

"Yes, this is Lisa. Who's this?"

"This is Carla."

Before I could get out my declaration of the time, she was already on it. "I'm so sorry for calling you this early. You must think I'm crazy."

Fred Sanford was now on my shoulder…Esther, you ugly AND crazy. Delirium had truly set in. Jesus sat on the other shoulder saying nothing. "No not at all. Are you ok?"

"Yeah, I, uh, well…I need some help."

I sat up.

"I actually need a little money. Or not money, necessarily. I need groceries."

The clouds were parting.

"You need groceries? You mean you need food?"

Carla did not give the impression that she was

hurting in any way or in need of anything. She wasn't fat by any means, but she certainly didn't look like she'd missed a meal. Always stylish, hair and nails done impeccably. She even had baby rhinestones on the tip of her pinkie nail.

"Yeah, I'm just a little short this month and thought maybe you could help a sister out."

"Of course."

"I thought maybe you could meet me at the Food for Less on Slauson at about seven a.m. I've got a session at nine and thought we could knock it out before then."

Without skipping a beat, I said "No problem. I'll pick you up at 6:45."

I had no problem believing that she really was desperate and how amazing it was that she called me out of all her friends. She must have really trusted me. Even considered me a home girl of sorts. As I lay my head back down for my remaining nanoseconds of sleep, my stomach felt a tinge of flutter. She is desperate, right? I am the only person she could have called, right? If I were wrong, it wouldn't be my first journey through gullible's travels. There was the health club that stole my $50 deposit—one day, a room full of stationary bikes and work out equipment, the next, an abandoned warehouse. There was Ben, the gropey frat guy who I believed really only wanted to listen to James Taylor albums behind his locked bedroom door. And then there was 'cuz', who promised not to scrape my teeth when spoon-feeding me her Icee but did it anyway. Nothing like brain freeze to let you know you're still alive. I so wanted to trust Carla. To connect with her. To be needed.

* * *

As we pulled up in front of the apartment complex somewhere near the corner of Roscoe and

Noble, I gave my face the once over in the car mirror. Lips, check, nose, check, wish I had a bit more eyeliner on but I'd left it on the bathroom sink. "Who's gonna be here?" I asked, readjusting my trademark bun on top of my head. Usually, it had three positions—high, innocent school girl look; straight back – sleek and sassy; and of course the ever so popular base-of-the-neck schoolmarm. When you've been wearing your hair the same way for 20 years, you have to find subtle ways of making it seem new. In one furious motion I yanked my scrunchie out, tethering my hair behind my right ear so the pony tail could cascade kinky waves down one shoulder. Get back, honky cat.

"I'm not sure. My buddy Kenny hooked it up. He's pretty wild but good people."

The complex was large and looming with very few street lights to illuminate the path. We walked in silence down a narrow passageway to the back of the building. Again, my gut started to flutter. Everything my parents or common sense ever taught me had disintegrated in those preliminary steps. Never relinquish control. Don't hang out at night. Always let someone know where you are. I stuffed those thoughts deep down into my "la la land" laundry basket as we rang the doorbell.

A thin, barefoot guy opened the door. He was wearing a white t-shirt and jeans. Not exactly what I'd call party attire. "Hey," he mumbled as he motioned for us to enter. He made sure to look behind us, I guess to see if anybody else was arriving.

"Hey," answered Carla. She linked arms with me. "Kenny, right?"

"Yeah, right" Odd, I thought this guy was her buddy. Now it seemed as though they were just meeting.

I looked past Kenny into the room. The place was bare, no furniture except for a couple three bean bags wedged in the corners. There was a kitchen counter to the immediate right with half full bottles of booze and cartons of juice. I was only about a couple of feet from the counter yet I couldn't read the labels. There was no light in the room, only a hallway light bulb jetting out from the side wall that allowed a few rays to spill into the living room where we were. Smoke hung heavy in the air swirling like a magic carpet with the slightest bit of movement. Something was droning in the background vaguely resembling music.

"You want a hook up?" as he pointed to the booze counter.

Carla sensed my reticence and piped up, "Sure we'll take two vodka tonics."

As Slim prepared the drinks I casually began to survey the room in detail. Didn't want to make any sudden moves that might disturb the chi. There were two guys standing across the room, shadowed due to lack of light, having a somewhat subdued conversation as they stared our way. There was one lad hunched over on the floor in front of one of the bags with his back to us.

"I'm gonna check on my homies. You ladies make yourselves comfortable."

As I raised my glass to feign sipping, I could see the hallway over the rim. It was packed. Guys leaning against the walls. Guys sitting on the floor with their knees in the chest. One guy staring straight ahead, maybe looking at us, maybe just concentrating on overworking his cigar. All guys. Something was moving slowly on the kitchen floor but I wasn't about to turn my head to see what it was. Fear started to lick the back of my neck.

"Carla, where the hell did you bring me?"

I noticed she had completely finished her drink.

"Chill out. The last thing you want these guys to think is that you're uptight. Relax." She dropped my arm, set down her empty glass and headed straight for the hallway.

The sea of arms and chests and torsos parted as she approached and then seamlessly closed in around her. Her face and hand appeared momentarily winking and waving as if to say, "Come on in, baby, the water is fine."

I made my way left to a small balcony. One of the guys who'd been whispering to his buddy broke off and reached for the screen door. "Hey, I'm Rod."

"Hey." I think that was my voice.

Rod was about my height, muscular. He looked like he could have been anywhere from 20 to 40. Young face with crows feet. Nice smile, yellow teeth. Full head of hair, Gheri curl. He too was wearing a white T and jeans.

"You look a little tense. Can I freshen your drink?"

"No, no . . . no, no, no." My God, please say something else besides no. "I mean yes. Yes I'm ok . . . thanks for asking but I'm fine."

"Cool. Why don't you wait out here. Catch some air. I'll be back in a minute." He slipped back inside.

The balcony was just as bare as the living room except for a bean bag and a medium sized suspicious looking plant. I plopped down in the bean bag nearly knocking over a phone sitting on a small weathered end table. I picked up the phone and called Bob.

"Hello?"

"Bob, it's me."

"Me who?"

"Me, Me! I need you to come get me."

"Where are you?"

"I have no idea."

Tears started to catch in the back of my throat. Jesus please, please. Was I still breathing? The flutter in my gut had turned to churning as I assessed my predicament. No cash, no ride, no idea where I was, house full of boys, bean bags. It was not looking good.

Do you know a cross?

Everything within me became silent. Still. Children of God should remember Whose they are. *Yes, I know a Cross.*

"Hello?" Bob repeated.

"Well, I kind of remember turning off of Sepulveda onto Roscoe. There's only one way to turn at that corner. I'll meet you somewhere on the block. And Bob?"

"Yeah."

"Bring a weapon."

Bob looked like a cross between Raggedy Andy and Howdy Doodie.

As I hung up the phone, I could see a torn up jean leg in my peripheral vision. "Who you callin'?" I looked up and it was Rod staring down at me, his eyes slightly glazed.

"A friend. I was trying to see if she wanted to join the party."

"Cool." He knelt down next to the bag and proceeded to unbutton my blouse.

"Excuse me, sir." I laughed a little but it was more to keep from getting sick to my stomach.

He leaned in really close and I could smell the stench of weed, whisky, and something metallic. "I know how to loosen you up."

I pushed up on either side of the bag as he pinned me down with his full weight. I couldn't hear anything except for the sound of cheap leather squeaking against the balcony floor. Scriptures came at me like jumbled flash cards. "Yea though I walk . . . ." "I can do all things . . . ." "A prudent person foresees the evil, and hides himself; but the simple pass on and are punished." OK Lord, as I bit what I'd hoped was a finger, we can talk about how dumb I've been later, just get me out of here.

I heard something screaming "Help me, Jesus" once, then twice. On the third time I realized the screaming voice was my own. Rod had bunched my blouse up in his fist and was reaching for my ankle. Maybe a wrestling move he'd learned on his high school team before he dropped out. He lost his balance and wedged himself between the side of the bag and balcony railing. I rolled off of the bean bag, through the screen door, and halfway into the middle of the living room before getting to my feet. As I closed the front door behind me, I looked back in the hall and it was empty. I didn't know where Carla was. I said a prayer for God to protect her as I hurdled a hedge. Bob was parked out in front.

"How did you find me?" as I slammed the car door shut.

"I don't know. Once I turned at the corner something told me to stop."

I turned my head toward the cool glass and let the tears run freely down into the crevices of my neck. Bob was nice enough to hold my hand but I didn't need him to. I knew exactly Who stopped him. I knew Who caused Rod to lose his balance. And I knew Who kept me. Yes, I know a Cross. I didn't want to think about all the things that could have happened. Just that they didn't. And that I was given a second chance to continue my path, wherever that might lead me.

I never hung out with Carla after that night. She called and left a few angry messages and made sure to sit as far away as possible in choir practice. Maybe she felt I'd abandoned her. But the only person I'd abandoned that night was the confused and timid follower within. Next time, I thought. There won't be a next time. Because next time, I'll remember who I am, and Whose I am.

Words in Rhyme to Fit the Time
Talent Seeks Its Highest Expression

Just as Black skin actors and entertainers were exposed
so a dunker or a behind-the-back passing star arose
With attitudes filled with confidence they did emerge
bolstered by fans, to the box office millions did surge
Critics cried hoodlums – saying ghetto image took sports to its brink
causing choir boy stature of sport's reputation to sink
Consumers countered, supplying the demand of sports fans today
far exceeds that of any sport thirst in the "lily white" day
where talent was honored through a segregated media norm
until God broke in His open competition forum

. . . .

Still Water Runs Deep

The stillness of arctic waters in their most placid state camouflages the unseen, unknown undercurrent of its environment. In our language, "still water runs deep" is an expression often used to indicate that the character of the person referred to is not as presented. In other words, what one sees is just the tip of the iceberg. Physical characteristics used to stereotype often give false impressions of the man behind the face. Wilt Chamberlain's public and private history demonstrated that it is unwise to get hung up on physical characteristics. Content of character is a more dependable measure. Choices over a period of time reveal an individual's camouflaged undercurrent. Wisdom chimes, "You can know a man or woman by what they produce."

On the night of March 2nd, 1962, I was the passenger in a car driven by a friend. Wilt asked me to drive back to New York City after a professional basketball game.

"Yeah, sure. Where are you parked?"

"Come over to our locker room after you shower."

"OK"

His company was a more interesting option than the team three-hour bus ride. Earlier, he had been a fierce foe whose athletic heroics rewrote the NBA record books. The feat remains the goal for future generations of elite basketball players to shoot for as they seek superstar status.

I smirked, "Whoa, Big Fella." The speedometer settled between 85 and 90 mph.

"I got you covered, Willie. You know I'm not going to do anything to hurt me." He flashed the infectious Big Wilt Chamberlain smile, supported by his normal confident, expressive body language. He stroked his Fu Man Chu and rambled on and on about a variety of current events during the first fifteen minutes, but surprisingly did not comment on his historic performance.

Cleveland Buckner, who had guarded Wilt along with every other center, quickly drifted into a noticeable snore in the back seat. Wilt had reluctantly agreed to his request for a ride back to New York.

"You got some sad players on your team."

The subject of the game had finally emerged.

I responded, "We would have whipped your butts if we hadn't concentrated so much effort on fouling you. Granted, you are the worst foul shooter in the history of the game, but to use intentional fouls as a game strategy is weak. 'Foul him! We don't want him to show us up. One hundred points would be catastrophic!' Our coach's neck muscles strained; his eyeballs pleaded, 'That's his team's goal: ONE HUNDRED POINTS.' No one thought that you, a 50% foul shooter at best, would make 28 out of 32 free throws. Everybody in that small gym was made conscious of the possibility every time you scored after halftime. Nobody had ever scored 100 points in one pro game. So what? What does it matter if you score 120? We're getting paid to beat your team, not you. It was ridiculous the last quarter." My eyes shifted. "You did find your groove out there tonight. You'll never shoot like that again. Never!"

He said nothing, but grinned like a donkey eating cactus.

Wilt and I were fierce competitors yet mutually respectful homeboys. The sound of tires intensified as we drove for a spell in silence, east on the Pennsylvania turnpike en route from Hershey toward New York City.

"When did you get this badder than bad brand new champagne-colored Cadillac, Wilt?"

"Ain't it fine? I borrowed it from Ike, my business manager. "

"The man must like you a lot." Silence reigned again.

Headlights of oncoming traffic highlighted Wilt's profile as the conversation turned introspective. "Willie, why do you think they imposed racial quotas? Many unbelievable brothers in ghettos around the country are ignored, not given a chance to make a living playing ball. The Knicks keep on losing rather than hire the city's best available talent. I don't get it. You've got some bad boys up there in Harlem. Shouting time will be when the best talent of all races and colors go at it in front of capacity crowds around the world. The ghetto game is a training ground for future stars. I predict that one day the demand of fans to be entertained – and to win – will pressure owners of the NBA teams to have bidding wars over Black talent."

I leaned toward him away from my wedge against the door. "Back to your put-down of my teammates. Johnny Green and Richie Guerin can start on most teams. The other guys are sincere people, but not professionally competitive. It has been good for me to get to know them. I'm more confident now than I've ever been. Players in this league are represented as the world's best. I'm not surprised the owners are uneasy. They don't want their attempts to control who succeeds exposed. As talented black-skinned men, we have to continue to exercise a lot of patience. But, back to your point, I admit, our team is not very deep in competitive talent."

Wilt quickly offered, "We opposing players can't believe the lameness in your teammates. They have a loser's attitude on and off the court. Every serious player in the ghetto knows that the final cut of your training camp supported the league's commitment to racial quotas. Before the season began, Brother Willie, your management knew in their hearts that better black-skinned manpower was available a few blocks away, uptown in Harlem. I have made it clear that my goal is to win the World Championship. Our owners are not innocent. They are in sync to attempt to hold back the inevitable. I'm not naïve. I keep NBA gold on the minds of my teammates. Eventually the owners' mindset will change. Competition for sports dollars will invigorate selfishness and greed motivation in the minds of the team owners. The prospect of overflow crowds and making lots of money from TV and marketing will open up the gates for young brothers. We do know how to put on a show, don't we?"

"You got that right." A nod and a loud "Amen!"

He continued, "Ghetto ball is open freedom of expression, the best kind of competition. It has produced a higher level of entertainment, but only Black folk have an opportunity to see the show. It's all confined to our house. We can't make no money playing in the inner city. Face it. We're entertainers, man, not a bunch of lightweight, overgrown jocks. That's what we Black players bring to the NBA. We are its under-realized potential. The foundation of pro sports' future greatness is being pioneered by owners who employ black skinned Americans in major sports. Me, Bill Russell, Oscar Robertson, Elgin Baylor, Jim Brown, Willie Mays, Hank Aaron, Jackie Robinson, Larry Doby and, yes, you too, Willie Naulls, are the future look of professional sports. We run faster, jump higher, are quicker, more spontaneous, and committed to imposing our will on anyone who challenges us – and all that other talk. They know it to be the truth. How did we get to be the best? Playing against each other in the ghetto. You have to be good to win in our inner city hot summer games. Everybody is airborne, suspended, 'til the best out-hangs the rest. You can't take weak stuff to the rim and not get a Wilson Burger for lunch. Why can't they open their eyes and see the advantage of using our abilities to fly?"

I cut in, "The few Black players in California universities were commanded not to dunk. 'It shows up the opposition. There's no place for dunking in basketball.' My coach emphatically stressed this point at halftime of one of our games. Let me share that revealing episode. As seconds ticked off the clock to end the first half, a teammate's shot ricocheted off the back part of the rim and bounced straight up. From underneath, I jumped up, elbows over the rim, grabbed the ball with both hands and slammed it through the basket behind my head."

"Naw, you didn't, Big Bad Willie Naulls." We slapped palms.

"Yeah, I did. Yeah! The fans went absolutely berserk – and for an extended period of time. Coach's remarks in the locker room clearly demonstrated the prevailing mental attitude of leading white basketball minds. 'Don't ever do that showboating again around here. This is not the place for that kind of basketball.' Coaches of Division I schools were obsessed with keeping the game under the rim. I dunked in junior high school, but it was frowned upon, so I retarded the growth of my God given talent. Our ghetto dunkers today practice it from a young age. Proficiency to perform any basketball maneuver is a cumulative conditioned skill. Dunking is an art form expression that combines genes, coordination, talent, timing, skill, desire and practice. You know that. The NBA doesn't promote dunking. Russ is the only player bold enough to do it every time he gets a chance. You rang the bell of freedom loud and clear tonight, my man. Your performance shouted, *'Let my people be free to express themselves.'* The black skinned men who endure the humiliation of racial quotas are today's signs of change. The NBA will face replacement if it continues its retarded expression. A new league that promotes freed basketball entertainers will surface to fulfill the demand of fans."

"You're right," Wilt said. "Open competition raises the bar of growth in our elite athletic world. I can put together a team of unemployed brothers today and beat most pro teams tomorrow. Especially the Knicks." He squealed a humorous laugh, then continued. "The best athletes, developed for the world's stage, will become the basis of real entertaining competition. I traveled around the world with the Harlem Globetrotters and learned one thing for sure. People everywhere know and appreciate talent and want to be entertained. If I owned an arena like Madison Square Garden, I could challenge the NBA for business. Eddie, our owner, and Abe Saperstein, who owns the 'Trotters, know in their hearts that I'm right. It scares them to think of a world in which we inmates would show them in need of a vision for the asylum. That might expose them as retarded. All I need is an arena that I own or control."

Wilt Chamberlain

with Harlem Globetrotters Owner Abe Saperstein

Following his First Team All American season with NCAA Basketball Finalists University of Kansas, Wilt left school early and became an immediate international superstar entertainer with the Globetrotters.

I hummed, "Brother. I didn't know you were so deep."

Wilt smiled a glance my way. "Keep it quiet. People who think I'm big, black, dumb and stupid will look around one day and I'll own what they were blind to see."

"Or fathom," I added.

He continued, "It matters what people write and say publicly about me. They paint me as a freak, a side show. These people don't know me! My own daddy don't know me. Of most importance, do the Black players respect me?" After a moment or two he continued, "That's a question, New York Willie. What do you think of Big Wilt? I'm averaging over 50 points and 25 rebounds a game. I value your friendship and opinion. You are a true pro who comes ready to ball every game. The best players, Black and White, respect you as an All Star. But, your team ain't that good. You know that," he chuckled. "Seriously, you're highly respected among the brothers, not only 'cause you can play – but – you know all the fine girls." He chuckled louder, then waited to know my thoughts.

Somewhat uneasy, "This car smells good, like a new car should," I said with emphasis. Then another pause. "You're a good friend to many people and a great athlete. Everybody concedes that as fact. All players, Black and White, look to you to negotiate salaries upward. You're in demand – more so than any athlete in any sport – and make more money than any player in the history of any league. So you got a lot of power – and responsibility – to influence higher contracts for everybody. Now, as far as basketball is concerned, if I were your coach, I'd demand that you change your mental attitude toward the game."

Wilt's brow furrowed over a glance. His eyes

pierced the pause, demanding that I continue.

"I'd demand that you take the ball to the hoop with authority. . ." I raised my arms and torso in a power pose, ". . . and dunk it every time. Your critics have duped you. You play like you're trying to prove to the world that you can shoot going away from the basket. You have proven yourself a proficient fade-away jump shooter. But you and your team would be unstoppable if you made a strategic mental adjustment." I leaned close to him. My breath singed the hair on the side of his head. "When you commit to impose all your power and will down through the hoop, on anyone who gets in your line of fire, then your force will demand respect from everybody. Your team will be unstoppable. Check out my man, Big Bad Bill Russell. He won two consecutive NCAA Championships in college. Now he's dunking his will on all of us as the Celtics relentlessly pursue NBA Gold."

Wilt became very quiet. I shut up and stared straight ahead, anxiously awaiting his response. My words were potentially training up the enemy's mental attitude. He obviously didn't need my help. He'd just scored 100 points against our team, hadn't he? I mumbled through clenched teeth to myself, *He may score 150 next time. Willie Naulls, are you crazy?*

"Nobody ever told me that to my face before," he offered. "People don't tell me the truth straight up like that." Obviously perturbed at his thoughts, he opened up even more as we turned north up the New Jersey Turnpike. "I hate it when people call me 'Wilt the Stilt.' Sarcastically they say, 'He's more height advantage than basketball ability.'"

"Yeah! I can definitely relate to what you're saying. My gripe is being called 'Willie the Whale' or, in some closed conversations, 'Willie the Big Black Whale.' It takes self control to not pick up one of those hemophiliac sports writers and throw him up in the second balcony." We both laughed out loud in relief of our suppressed thoughts. I continued, "The obvious insecurity expressed through some sports reporters has developed a superior veneer in most Black athletes."

Wilt sighed, took a deep breath. "Putting up an insular mental wall has buffered me to ignore insensitive comments. My parents directed me to restrain myself when under any kind of attack. A wise friend in South Philly said, 'Public hanging and castration of Black men has taken on a new, written, form in sports.' Therefore, I note all their words to expose the character of the monsters we're dealing with."

"Wilt, We are the crest of the wave of change, a new opportunity and beginning. Black men in sports are leading the way of practical integration. For the first time in our history, Black men are free to compete against White men for positions which pay a salary. That's a meritorious fruit of the civil rights struggle in this country. The law of supply and demand of the athletic business world will increasingly open up opportunities for Black men to get paid for doing something we enjoy. That's what our parents prayed for, isn't it? Sports writers and commentators are 'Stay in your place, Black boy' hit men. Fortunately, our parents raised us to get going when the attacks get tough. We know we have to be better. That's our mental advantage."

"Willie, I didn't know you thought as I do about these things." We slapped hands.

After a long pause, Wilt asked, "Do you think most Black pro players can see the importance of making a commitment to be positive role models? Every one of us can open up opportunities for competitively talented brothers. As I said before, writers influence negative public opinion about Black athletes. For that reason, I don't like the image they've influenced people to have about me."

"Laugh all the way to the bank, Wilt. People around the country are in awe of you. In college track you high-jumped over seven feet, ran the quarter-mile in less than 48 seconds and were All-World in everything you attempted in sports. No one can justify not acknowledging you as one of the greatest athletes who ever lived, Black or White. As my mom told me, 'Sticks and stones may break bones, but….' Sports writers' words? Give me a break. Words can affect you only when you allow them inside to fester and grow."

Wilt's thoughts shifted. "I have a close relationship with our owner, Eddie. He boasts commitment to grooming me to be an NBA team owner, but I suspect he's just trying to divert my attention from asking for more money. They forget, on occasion, that I'm Black and represent all Black players. Eddie violates their code and takes me to informal league meetings. On one occasion an owner blurted out, 'Willie Naulls' reputation is bad for our business. Does it bother anybody else that he's seen in every league city with beautiful White women?'" Wilt paused and smirked my way, "What do you think about that, Willie Naulls? Didn't your coach in college teach you to fear the negative reactions of White fans when you walk around publicly with White girls?"

I snapped, "Ever since I was in grammar school 99.9% of the people around me were White. I don't specifically seek out White folk. My teammates have always been mostly White. From junior high through college, we united as a team against all other schools. Most opponents were all White; some were integrated, and very few were all Black. But –

they were equally our enemy. I have been a star all of my athletic life. My teammates, classmates, coaches, teachers and administrators have been and continue to be predominantly White. As a pro, wherever I go, more than any other Black athlete known to me, I am pursued by White people. They have voted me to be their leader and representative on every stage upon which I have been cast. I've been the first black-skinned man to lead in many integrating environments. Sports team integration is leading the way for race relations in our world to liberate people to freely choose associations. The owners you mentioned, whomever they represent, are threatened and speak sweeping speculations, in an attempt to spread fear. I suspect their goal is to keep players divided to manipulate salaries. Their myopic opinion is their problem. It mirrors the worst attitude of insecure White males – not limited to those who live in the South – toward Black men." Raising my shoulders upward and backward for maximum sarcastic emphasis, I continued. "They're jealous because my female associates are university educated, articulate, highly motivated, quality, mostly religious, physically beautiful women, who view me as a man first, not a skin color."

We slapped hands and roared in agreement yet again. "You got that right, Big Fella," Wilt said. "You gotta share just one fine girl's number with your man Wilty. I am a strong relief man you know." He rocked back and forth laughing out of control, slapping the steering wheel with his hands.

After calming down, he got pensive again. "Seriously, Willie, when you retire, don't ever look for a job in the NBA. These close-minded men who run this league hate you and your suave, best-looking, best-dressed-man-in-sports, new Negro persona. They don't wish you well. And that Haskell guy has really got a thorn in his butt thing about you. Did you dare to challenge the NBA's authority to use your name and picture on Bubble Gum cards without your permission? Have you forgotten your place?" he smirked. His eyes shone glee. "Haskell knew he messed up when he authorized a company to market your image without your signature." Wilt leaned over toward me to emphasize his point. "Hear me, Naulls. He don't like you. You exposed him to be condescending and disrespectful. The whole world got a look at his dirty drawers. Even Howard Cosell asked me about it. Black stud, he would like you out of the league. Why do you think you don't get the press you deserve. Eddie told me he's the one who filters your record with his dirty rags. You average over 25 points and 15 rebounds per game – a career of double digits with the Knicks. Yet, the only thing I read about you is that you're soft on defense or something else subjective. And they publicly question where your head is when you're supposed to be concentrating on the game. Tell the truth, my main man. Do you be looking – like they say – for pretty girls in the stands when you're supposed to be concentrating on the game?"

I answered him by laughing out loud.

He leaned his head back with mouth wide open and roared without restraint again as he raised his hand for another slap.

"Looking at girls in the crowd is not unique to me. Most players do, including you!" We continued to laugh from down deep. "I've never been confronted verbally by an owner. They usually stare and ask polite questions, but never a confrontation. Listen to this. In the midst of a team Christmas party at the Copa Cabana in mid-town Manhattan, a teammate asked, 'Is your date a White girl, Willie. I mean it don't matter to me. She sure is fine – but – is she?' I answered, 'On family occasions like tonight's, you White boys should pay closer attention to your wives and stop drooling over my women friends.' He smiled in reaction to the inflection in my voice. 'Yeah, it don't matter to me, Willie, but she sho' is fine. My wife said she thought she had seen her in a Hollywood movie.' His eyes glowed as he drew me nearer. 'You know, we'll be in L.A. next month!' I placed my arm around him and whispered in his ear, 'Down, boy. Calm down. This is a time for your wife, not mental fantasy.' He laughed hysterically and slapped his knees with both hands, his head moving from side to side, mumbling, 'She sho' is fine, Willie. My, my, my – she sho' is fine.'"

Wilt and I slapped hands over and over, letting the good times out as we rolled along, consistently near 95 mph. He was the original "weighted foot."

With sternness, to emphasize his point, "I'll tell you again, the owners don't like you. They don't appreciate your West Coast liberated, self-confident, good-English-talking, playboy image reputation. You, Willie Naulls, are the first player in the NBA with a unique background. You're comfortable with White people and have lived among them. Contrary to most of our experiences, you've lived in an integrated, White situation most of your life. Let me give an example of why you're my hero." Another smirk. "The talk among the owners around the NBA last summer was your contract negotiations with the Knicks. Everybody was shocked that you told the owner – and general manager – and coaches to observe the mistletoe on your coattail." Wilt hesitated. "Willie, tell the truth. Did you tell them, 'Don't ever talk to me again in that demeaning tone. I'm not a mule busting straight rows for you – like on a Southern plantation. If you can't talk to me like a man, each of you can take a basketball, deflate it, and you know where you can stuff it.' Did I hear it right, Big Fella?" He smiled confidently. "Don't forget. The NBA keeps a record of your every move. Watch your back. They don't mean you well. You are unofficially black-balled – or is it white-balled? Whatever you choose, it ain't good."

I pondered his words and advice. The truth from his perspective evoked discomfort. "Thank you for filling me in with that privileged information. Not many Black athletes hear the truth about what owners really think. As I said before and reiterate, everything they do is designed to divide and increase control. My position: Any crumb they would throw my way to lure me to be their stay-in-my-place Negro, I vehemently reject. Our brothers and sisters are dying in the south as we speak so we can have the right to choose to develop into who we were created to be, individually. I refuse to live in fear of anybody's subjective approval. I'm a man first. I am covered with black skin. And I am proud of my heritage. I . . ." pounding my chest for emphasis ". . . have chosen to play professional basketball. I know why I'm in the league. Because I can do our game better than most and as well as anyone who has ever tried. I know many strong White men out west who could eat these NBA owners up as snacks. They wish me well from their platforms of power. I've learned to be ready and prepared to race through the door that opportunity opens. These power hungry misers here in the NBA are still carrying their lunches in paper bags. Their fear tactics don't scare me. I'm a man first – who competitively earned the privilege to play basketball in the NBA. Thank you again for the confidential information."

We slapped hands once again. Wilt oozed respect, convicted by my words. "You're all right with me, my brother."

It was well after two in the morning when we arrived at my home in Montclair, New Jersey. I declined his invitation to celebrate with his anxiously awaiting fans in Harlem. Although the offer to continue our rap was a pleasant thought, I did not feel up to the bombardment of Harlem's late night 100-point-game chatter. He continued to talk for an extended time about Wilt Chamberlain, the man, his dreams.

"This looks like a nice community, Naulls. Beautiful two-story homes. Looks like wealthy folk live here. Any of us own these homes?"

"Yeah. Hawthorne Place is a quiet street. It connects Lower and Upper Montclair. In the '30s and '40s, this was reported to be the richest town per capita in the USA. Lower Montclair was home to the maids and butlers of the wealthy residents of Upper Montclair. Descendants of slaves who migrated here from the South sent their children away to college, paid for by their domestic wages. That educated generation returned to our town as legal, business, education and medical professionals. Eventually they challenged the covenants and conditions of property ownership and purchased homes wherever they chose in Montclair. It's a great and inspiring story."

"Yeah, that's interesting. I dream of becoming the first basketball player to buy and use a race horse as a tax deduction." His spirit perked. "To pioneer Black businesses wherever I am is a passion in my heart."

"Thank you for the piece of yourself you have shared with me.

"It was a mutual pleasure. Oh! Will you please call my club and tell them I'm on my way?" he said, and departed east toward Harlem.

Wilt Chamberlain's non-athletic decisions caused the sports world to take notice and give an attentive look beneath his Still Waters. He owned his own Harlem night club, Big Wilt's Smalls Paradise, the largest in town. He demanded one half of the gross from summer exhibition games in which he played. At half time he counted receipts with the promoter, then deposited his 50%-of-the-gross cash into the trunk of his guarded car before returning to play the second half. His dream of ownership of a race horse to depreciate came true. Spooky Cadet was that horse's name.

He moved to Los Angeles to play with his second World Championship team, the Lakers. He owned and depreciated apartment buildings to increase his net spendable cash before it was fashionable for athletes to do so. In the 1970s he built a palatial mansion on top of Bel Air, home location of Hollywood's rich and famous. People told him he was crazy to invest a reputed million dollars cash on a custom built home. They speculated, "Wilt doesn't know what he's doing." Today that home is considered unique, even in "the land of fruits and nuts," valued at fifteen to twenty million dollars.

Wilt called me from his Harlem office later that morning. I could hear his friends and fans in the background as they continued to celebrate his 100-point Night In Flight. The conversation began where we had closed down. "I am sensitive and aware of all the negative comparisons of me to Bill Russell. Sports writers portray me as one who selfishly strives to score a lot of points. They call me and our team losers for not winning the NBA championship every year. Hear me loud and clear, Naulls. When I leave this game of pro basketball, I will be its top scorer and rebounder of all time. My final all-time statistics, totals and averages, will be the only thing people remember about me. Long after our playing days are over, that's all they will talk about until some descendants of ghetto families make them forget us. I will also be a world champion before I retire. And – I heard you loud and clear. Wilty is going to the hoop with all my might and will every time there's an opening."

We shouted a hearty "Yeah!"

He paused. "By the way, my friend. Our soul chatter last night was between you and me, and no one else, until I'm dead. Deal?"

"To honor my word is my name, and loyalty is my game." I assured him he could count on my discretion and silence.

"Dig you later."

During his career, he got every rebound he could and scored every point he could. He played as many minutes of every game he could for as many years as he could, until his body told him, "I'm too tired to carry the freight any more." Wilt Chamberlain retired as the NBA's "greatest of all time." He became its most proficient player and established professional career scoring and rebounding records. He even led the NBA in assists one year. On a talk show interview after his retirement he challenged his critics with a question: "Where are the geniuses who said Wilt Chamberlain is a loser? Check out my world championship rings from two cities," he boasted in fun.

Wilt's prophecy, sworn to Covenant silence, was right on that night. Black skinned professional athletes filled ten of the eleven positions on the 2007-08 roster of the World Champion Boston Celtics led by an African-American former player and now Coach of the Year. Our parents' prayers were answered as all athletes are now meritoriously rewarded for developing the talent with which God has blessed them to glorify Him. Some – like the NBA's Miami Heat superstar Dwyane Wade and 2007 Heisman Trophy winner and quarterback of the 2008 NCAA National Champion Florida Gators Tim Tebow – give the Lord the glory for their success.

The ride and the private fellowship are exclusively ours. In that regard, Wilt Chamberlain and Willie Naulls are Brothers, In the Night of His 100 Point Flight, Forever. **Still Water Runs Deep.**

NBA Top 20 Scorers • 1961-62

Player	G	FG	FT	PTS	PPG
Wilt Chamberlain (Philadelphia)	80	1597	835	4029	50.4
Elgin Baylor (Los Angeles)	48	680	476	1836	38.3
Walt Bellamy (Chicago)	79	973	549	2495	31.6
Bob Pettit (St. Louis)	78	867	695	2429	31.1
Oscar Robertson (Cincinnati)	79	866	700	2432	30.8
Jerry West (Los Angeles)	75	799	712	2310	30.8
Richie Guerin (New York)	78	839	625	2303	29.5
Willie Naulls (New York)	75	747	383	1877	25.0
Cliff Hagan (St. Louis)	77	701	362	1764	22.9
Jack Twyman (Cincinnati)	80	739	353	1831	22.9
Hal Greer (Syracuse)	71	644	331	1619	22.8
Tom Heinsohn (Boston)	79	692	358	1742	22.1
Paul Arizin (Philadelphia)	78	611	484	1706	21.9
Bailey Howell (Detroit)	79	553	470	1576	19.9
Wayne Embry (Cincinnati)	75	564	356	1484	19.8
Gene Shue (Detroit)	80	580	362	1522	19.0
Bill Russell (Boston)	76	575	286	1436	18.9
Sam Jones (Boston)	78	596	243	1435	18.4
Rudy LaRusso (Los Angeles)	80	516	342	1374	17.2
Dave Gambee (Syracuse)	80	477	384	1338	16.7

G=Games FG - Field Goals FT = Free Throws
PTS - Points PPG = Points Per Game

Freedom

For Freedom to ring in your heart's tower
God's Word must reign supreme every hour
Don't yield to the world's temptation's flight
Exalt God! Use the Holy Spirit's Might
For God grants Freedom to those who believe
who stand on His Word, have Freedom indeed
What price Freedom? Exchange death for Living?
Christ's sacrifice the cost in God's GIVING!
Freedom begins, conception with thought
Agreement with God's Word, a saint is caught
Before Christ paid the price to loose sin's grip
there was no hope – death was man's one-way trip
Shout! -– Let the Voice of Freedom ring
for eternity – may the saints sing
blessed praises to Christ Jesus
Let the voices of Freedom ring

Believe to See

Cancer – Be Damned!

"You have Stage III colon cancer."

These words are etched in Gina's memory. The doctor's proclamation confirmed her worst fear, but began her new journey on the road of prayer and faith in God.

At the of five, her body had been invaded by scarlet fever. It erupted through the skin, inflamed by a fever greater than 104 degrees. A month's duration caused her shoulder length blonde hair to fall out. As a young Catholic, she had been taught to acknowledge God, but was not mature enough to consciously know how to call on Jesus for healing.

For her daughter, Anna prayed daily for God's mercy. Because of her own difficult childhood, she and Gina had a troubled relationship. Yet for more than three weeks she never left Gina's side, even sleeping with her to calm her fears as skin sloughed off onto the sheets. Anna's husband, Alfredo, and son, Emilio, had moved in with her in-laws during the quarantine period. They came back to the small three-bedroom rented house occasionally to bring gifts from family members and from Alfredo's co-workers at the River Front carpet mill. Alfredo's green eyes brimmed with tears at the sight of his precious Gina. He felt inadequate, unable to help her. Every departure was dramatic and painful as both father and daughter fought fatalistic thoughts.

During a visit from the local physician, the exhausted Anna pleaded, "Doctor, my little girl is miserable, near death. Her hair is falling out; her skin is scorched and dried and broken. Day and night we call on God for healing. Is there nothing more we can do?"

A gleam of hope sparkled in his eyes. "There's a new experimental drug that's not yet on the market. It's untested and there are risks." Anna stood, faced him eyeball to eyeball. Surely he had the answer to their prayers. "Your daughter may have adverse side effects. The drug may not help at all."

Tears of hope flushed down to her chin. Her voice desperately cried out, "We want our daughter back to her normal happy self. Look at her. How much worse could the side effects be? Please, give her the new drug. Please, Doctor."

Twenty-four hours later, satan was stilled by God's wisdom in a syringe filled with penicillin. The month long ordeal had taken a mental and physical toll, for Gina was confined to an insulated bedroom. The beginning of the healing process inspired a confession from the abundance of Gina's neophyte heart and soul: "I don't know you, God, but I will serve you the rest of my life." Her entire being breathed a deep sigh of relief and thanksgiving.

She glimpsed herself in the bathroom mirror. A tear drained through a healing scab at the side of her left eye and trickled down onto her trembling blistered lips. "Mama, I feel better today. Will I look better tomorrow?"

"You're going to be just fine, Gina." Anna opened her arms and drew her sobbing daughter to her bosom and rocked her until she slept.

God's Spirit inspired more indelible imprints on Gina's young soul. In the morning she awakened with a message from God in her heart, "Always come to Me in your child-like faith."

The word quickly spread throughout their small Italian Catholic community. God's divine intervention into the life of their heritage was exalted.

Gina had been born in 1940 in the small town named Amsterdam, 30 miles west of Albany in upstate New York. The many windmills in the area are a testament to its Dutch foundation. Its population of 25,000 was comprised mostly of separate communities of Italian and Polish Catholics, although there was also one Protestant church in town during her childhood.

Large Italian families, all Catholic, lived around their home. Her mother's relatives lived in an impoverished community on the south side of Amsterdam. Anna's parents, Federico and Rosaria, had been born into uneducated families in Sicily. Both entered the United States through Ellis Island and eventually moved to Amsterdam, as did many others from Italy. Life was difficult for them as only eleven of their fourteen children survived the first year of life. Gina's paternal grandparents told her about the "sunny part of Italy" where their families had lived. Alfredo's father, Ricardo, had come through Ellis Island as well and had married Natalia, a Queen of the May Day Parade who had been born in New York City. They lived on the more affluent east side of Amsterdam, just across a bridge over the Mohawk River from Gina's home.

Fear prevailed over Gina's early life. When she was 19, her beloved father died of cancer at 51. Later, her brother died of cancer at 39. She watched Emilio give up after he was told the tumor had metastasized to his brain. He chose not to undergo chemotherapy or radiation and died six weeks after surgery. Gina tried hard to minister to him on his death bed when he asked her, "How does a person prepare to die?"

She didn't know. All the years of going to church, and no one had ever taught her anything to prepare to answer that question. She embraced guilt thinking she had failed her brother. Not only that. She was convinced that she would get cancer as well.

Gina had considered committing her life to becoming a nun throughout adolescence because she desired to serve God. Ambivalence confused which path to take. At 25 years of age, while working in upstate New York, she knelt at the altar at church to pray for guidance. "God, if there is someone anywhere in this world for me, please send him. You know that I don't care for the men I've been raised around."

Six months later, a nuclear engineer named Stanley was hired by the company which employed Gina. He had been born in Mobile, Alabama, but moved to Houston as a child. Now the Navy sent him to wherever they needed him. His gentle and considerate manner impressed Gina to conclude that he was a faithful, dedicated man of integrity.

Stanley and Gina were married six months after they met and lived in many locations in the United States and abroad as dictated by the Navy. His family had been strong Christians for generations and they attended Protestant churches, but for the next twenty years Gina continued to practice Catholicism. It wasn't until the age of forty-five that she experienced the baptism of the Holy Spirit while studying the Book of John at Bible Study Fellowship and was born again.

At fifty-one, Gina began having gastrointestinal symptoms, including bleeding. The doctors at the medical center took two years to finally diagnose the problem. On 14 July 1993, they were able to announce a final conclusion.

"You have Stage III colon cancer, Gina, and it has probably penetrated the wall of the colon and involved other organs as well. We would like to schedule your surgery right away."

The word "cancer" traumatized Gina. Her worst

fear was realized. Almost immediately the Spirit of God led her to specific Scriptures. "This sickness will not end in death. No, it is for God's glory so that God's Son may be glorified through it." A calm entered into her mind while meditating on God's Word.

A friend at the Methodist church Gina and Stanley attended at that time was head of the pharmacy at M.D. Anderson Cancer Center. He advised her not to rush into a surgical procedure. "I think you should get a second opinion. I can help you set that up. They have a program second to none at our hospital."

"Thank you. I receive your counsel as from the Lord."

The new doctors estimated that the baseball-size tumor had probably been growing for fifteen years. "We recommend six weeks of chemotherapy and then radiation prior to surgery. We will not know whether the tumor has penetrated the wall of the colon until surgery, but we are optimistic. How about you, Gina?"

"Doctor, my prayer is that, if God so wills to heal me, He will give me a quality life, not just a quantity."

Stanley continued to be the rock Jesus had sent to Gina. During the ordeal, he spent time in the library to learn as much as he could to interact with the doctors as her advocate.

Gina praised God for directing her to M.D. Anderson. The many incredible things that happened there were faith builders. The Word of God became her constant companion.

A card from one of her prayer partners encouraged with the words of Psalms 41:3: "The Lord will sustain him on his sickbed and restore him from his bed of illness." She knew God was speaking to her, using people with whom she fellowshipped.

Although she had borne three children, Gina had never received an intravenous line or stitches. But this was a different situation entirely. She was required to have a long intravenous line placed deep into her body in order to receive chemotherapy. She was terrified.

"Come with me, Gina." As they turned into another long hallway, the nurse directed her to an area past several waiting rooms. "Your procedure, scheduled for the late afternoon, will be done in this room, number 707."

On the wall of the hospital room was a picture of a beautiful ocean scene. Painted from a vantage point on top of a hill, the mighty Pacific splashed across the canvas as waves carved the rocks into unique patterns and beaches settled serenely along the coastline. Gina envisioned Jesus in the picture and received His peace. Again, Scripture came forth out of her heart: "He tends His flock like a shepherd. He gathers the lambs in His arms and carries them close to His heart; He gently leads those that have young."

After placement of the IV, the nurses left for the day. Gina was later taken to have an x-ray to check that the long line's placement was true. A man entered the room and said, "The good news is that I'm here to help you. The bad news is that the long line didn't go in and I will have to do it again." He continued, "You will always remember my name, Jamaal, because I'm the best."

When Gina was being prepped the next day to start chemo, she told the nurses, "I want to thank Jamaal. He did such a good job inserting the IV. Is he working today?"

The women looked confused. "There's no IV nurse at the hospital named Jamaal." Gina smiled, convinced that God had sent her an angel.

She always remembers the exact date of her first operation, 27 September 1993. While being prepared for surgery, she pleaded with the surgeon, "Will you please remove my appendix as well."

"This is a long, serious operation, Gina. I don't usually do elective procedures at the same time."

"I don't know why, but I have a nagging thought about my appendix and can't get it out of my mind. Please remove it," she persisted.

In the recovery room, the doctor revealed the results of his exploratory surgery. "The chemo and radiation did their job. The tumor had shrunk by seventy-five percent. It had gone right to the wall of the colon but never penetrated it, so a colostomy was not required. And your premonition was right! I removed the appendix and there was a precancerous polyp in it!"

Gina's face flushed. Her eyes drained, "Thank you, Jesus!"

At three in the morning after the surgery, Gina awoke in intense pain. She lifted her head, saw a bright light in the room and experienced the Lord's presence. All the faces of her prayer partners passed before her.

God said to her heart, "You're going to make it. It will be hard, but you're going to make it. And I'm going to use you."

Gina wept deeply.

A nurse came in and said, "Why are you crying? Are you in pain?"

"Did you see the bright light?" Gina responded.

"No. You may have just been visited by the Lord Jesus for His work," said the nurse, a missionary worker.

Gina smiled and perked up. "What's that perfume you're wearing? The aroma is wonderful."

The young Filipina smirked a sarcastic response.

"It surely is not me. I've worked a double shift and have been on my feet for quite a few hours."

They laughed together, then abruptly sobered with the same thought, *I wonder what the fragrance was in the alabaster jar when Mary anointed the Lord Jesus and wiped his feet with her hair?*

Six months later, after a second surgery to take down the ileostomy, Gina began six more months of chemotherapy. Eight years after her initial diagnosis, the doctors released her from their care. The recommended follow-up has shown no recurrence. She continues to praise the Lord.

Gina confesses she was a fearful person and thought she would die at fifty-one. Two years later, when she received the diagnosis, she felt strong enough to say, "OK, cancer has attacked my body but I'm not going to die. I have God's Word to stand on. So, cancer be damned!" Her faith brought her through four operations and two different rounds of chemotherapy. God's Word sustained her and sustains her still. She continues to walk by faith and not by sight.

Gina's witness and life story are a testimony to the faithfulness of God to His Word. She often quotes Jesus: "Did I not tell you that if you just believed, you would see the glory of God?"

In the Process

In the Process
of ongoing themes
stitching the seams
of the garment of life to wear
Striving and working
weaving the character
illuminates the cross to bear

Midday slumber
lack of focus is the number
How important is the work – to do?
Tallying what's abounding
encouraging the floundering
like scores of others in life's zoo

Misguided muscles
en route to their tussles
thoughts of pleasure being their guide
Fad laden dreams
chasing temporary schemes
stopping to let a breath hitch a ride

Tomorrow's thinking
hard to see through the blinking
on the road of challenge's pursuit
Evolving maze of procession
dawning a symphonic repression
Don't want to be another loser's recruit

In the Process
is worked out through moving
whatever God wants you to be ensuing
off the stalemate of your indecision's coup-ing
Don't let idleness's progress remain
stuck in the mire of your indecision's domain
Walk in God's faith of In the Process's Proclaim

AHA Moment

"Come on, people!" I leaned on the horn. The driver in front inched forward through the green light. The culprit's beady eyes glared through his rearview mirror. That wasn't a smirk, was it?

"I don't believe this!" Both hands crashed down on the steering wheel, my teeth grinding behind a twisted snarl.

Jonathan giggled from the rear seat, his two-year-old feet kicking with glee against the back of the armrest near my elbow. He often was amused by my exasperation. "I don bweev dis!" he exclaimed in perfect mimicry. His arms flailed and his eyes beamed like headlights for my approval and participation.

The gridlock of cars could add at least 20 minutes to the commute and I was late already. A premonition of my day at work came to mind, not unlike those shared survivor stories of near death experiences when their entire lives flash before their eyes. A sneer here, a chortle there, a raised eyebrow there, a sympathetic yet nervous smile over there. The elite twenty- to thirty-something high-producing jet set at work had no idea what my mornings were like. I'd been up since five a.m. – washing, cleaning, showering, dressing, feeding, spilling, showering again, dressing Jonathan, cleaning oatmeal off his shirt, dressing Jonathan again—did they care? Not in the least. By the time I belted up in the car, I was in a full sweat. My antiperspirant would be working overtime today. That is, if I even remembered to put it on. My kingdom for some Ban Roll On. I thought about the call I'd have to make to Corporate HR to explain my tardiness and negotiate leaving late rather than the reduction in personal time off. Not unlike splinter removal.

To hell with them. I'm frickin doing the best I can, I thought. Or so I thought I thought. Jonathan rarely missed a chance to practice his budding language skills. Of course this sentence, which I must have uttered, he heard quite clearly. It was just a plethora of vocabulary splendor.

"Hell, hell, hellllla la LA LA"

"No sweetie, that's not a nice…"

"FRICK…FRICKIN"

"Jonathan, stop please, Love"

"FRICKIN HELL"

"JONATHAN, STOP!"

"….Hell…"

I winced as I saw Oprah yank the Mother of the Year award out of my clutches. The crowd booed. My pastor just shook his head. Is this God's Holy Spirit-filled expression to the world? A defensive smile of guilt crept into my consciousness.

As Jonathan did whenever I deigned to raise my voice to him, he proceeded to cry, his face twisted and pinched with little droplets squeezing out of the corners of his eyelids. I patted my own droplets that had begun to bead up on my forehead.

The smirker had long since moved on and had been replaced by a Methuselah on wheels. I mused under a breath, I don't think I'm ever getting to work today. I could barely see her little silver meringue of Aqua Velvet and curls peaking above the headrest. I took the opportunity to plunge my fist into my purse, desperately searching for Jonathan's bubbles. Anything to divert his hysteria, I thought.

"Sshhhh…sweet love, mommy is sorry she raised her voice."

Jonathan ramped it up. I guess he was teaching

me a lesson.

Eureka, the bubbles.

"Jonathan, how would you like to blow some bubbles?"

His bellowing instantly ceased. His hands reached, stretching forward his pudgy little digits, damp with mucus and tears. Ahh, the joys of Motherhood.

The traffic finally opened up and I took an opportunity to make up some lost time. Flipping on the radio, I weaved in an out of cars like a pro not only passing up Methuselah but Smirky as well. I was just in time to catch the end of the latest Hollywood buzz. "…The Travolta family has asked the public to respect their privacy at this tragic time."

Travolta? What happened? Travolta was a household name for my generation. I was practically spoon fed on "Welcome Back Kotter" and "Saturday Night Fever." At one point in my young adult life, I could dance all the moves, recite, and sing verbatim the words to "Grease," both Sandy and Danny's parts. Lynn would know what was up, I thought as I reached for my cell phone.

"Les count the bubbles mommy."

"Hey Lynn, what's up? ... Mmmm… Uh huh… Listen, I heard something about Travolta tragedy on the radio just now. Do you know what happened? Oh... Wow… Man…how old was he? Sixteen?! Lord…all right, I can't really talk now I'm trying to get into the office. I'll call you later. Bye bye."

His son is gone. I shut the radio off and looked through the car window into the sky. It was overcast and heavy with big billowy clouds that swirled like black and grey marbled ice cream. I felt a deep pressure in my chest begin to creep in. It was growing, seeping into my gut and wrapping around both hips. It took a minute to realize it was grief. I didn't know this man, nor did I know his family. But I felt like I did – felt like he was my childhood buddy. He was a celebrity, but inside, he was my friend and I was so sad for his loss.

"Mommy, les count the bubbles" Jonathan blew what must have been at least 30 bubbles my way. They darted and danced on the windshield in front of me. Two popped on my wrist.

"1, 2, 3, 4, 5, 6, 7. There are so many, sweetie."

His torrential tear-fest was a faint memory now, and he beamed with delight that we could count together. I saw Jonathan at the podium giving his valedictorian speech, shaking hands with the headmaster and accepting his diploma.

"Les count the bubbles, Mommy."

Somehow I had made it to the parking lot of Jonathan's school. The lot was deserted. All the kids had been dropped off at least a half an hour earlier. I turned the car off and got out. Instead of unlatching Jonathan from his car seat, I suddenly had an impulse to get in next to him. He was thrilled.

"Les count, les count."

I thought of the Travoltas. About how they had been on vacation with their son. Hours earlier, they may have been at a buffet table, in their cabin playing cards, maybe sitting by the pool. Not knowing that those moments would be the last for their son. I rubbed Jonathan's cheek with my thumb.

"Blow, Jonathan. Blow more bubbles, sweetie."

He shrieked with excitement and blew columns of sudsy bubbles into the air. The car filled with bubbles, moving, popping, kissing our cheeks, our hands. 25, 50, 82…

"COUNT, MOMMY, COUNT!"

100, 200, 315…

The school and parking lot drifted up and stuck on the ceiling of the car. The office and coworkers floated by, then popped on the dashboard. I saw in one bubble Jonathan on the little scale that read 9 pounds 12 ounces; in one, the lake at sunset from my balcony; in another, my parents waiting for us at the airport baggage claim in Texas. I held the family Christmas tree in one hand, and a beach in Carmel in the other.

"Les count the bubbles Mommy." The many many bubbles in our lives are gifts to delight in no matter how brief the experience. God's bubbles. I kissed Jonathan on the nose and he took the wand and wiped it against my blouse, leaving a nice sudsy wet spot.

Nevertheless, Lord, Thy Will Be Done

I gave up my business empire and all of its
reward
and turned to the road less traveled, pledging
my life to be in accord
with a new set of values, raising my Standard
to be
God's Word manifested, through His Vision
entrusted to me

. . . .

And the Lord Said . . . .

I knew the epiphany was real. It was God and He didn't leave me any "Yeah, but" room.

"Get out of business!"

That's a command! The driver of the car in the next lane blared his horn to remind me why traffic lanes are painted on freeways.

"Better prepare yourself
to minister My Word."

The unexpected Voice continued, in anticipation of my question.

Another blare. The same driver raced past, now on my left, screamed and made gestures.

"Tell people what great things
I have done in your life."

Then – silence. My car settled on the right shoulder of the southbound San Diego Freeway in Culver City, California.

"What was that," I asked out loud. "Who are you?"

No answer . . . .

After some time, I continued the drive back to my Ford dealership in Hawthorne.

"Good morning, Mr. Naulls. You look like you've just seen a ghost." Carlos, our customer service writer, commented on an apparently unusual expression on my face as he took the car keys.

"How's business? All the service bays appear to be filled. Has it been that way all day?"

He smiled, "Yes, sir. All the mechanics have been non-stop since seven a.m. That's six hours – non-stop."

"Great. Is Chuck back from lunch?"

"He just went into his office."

"Thank you. The new paint job on the buildings looks spectacular, doesn't it? Our color choice of stark white with royal blue trim around the top perimeter really makes the place look alive. You do know that blue is true UCLA Bruin."

"Yeah. It does look great. But many of your customers are USC fans." I acknowledged the wisdom in his words and laughed as we parted in opposite directions.

The back lot was filled with shipments of new cars and overflowed with fleet trucks and vans. I picked up my pace across the separated previously owned and new car acreage.

"Good morning, Mr. Naulls." Salesmen smiled at the boss and bowed heads in respect of the perceived power of my position as co-owner. Their small talk didn't register. My mind was preoccupied. *What happened back there on the freeway?*

Chuck's door was ajar. "Come on in, Willie. Well, we gonna get the Lincoln-Mercury dealership in Oxnard or not? When will the new auto mall be completed?" His brow furrowed. "Are you feeling OK?"

I closed the door, walked around his desk and sat down. Looking past him through the floor-to-ceiling one-way window, I could see the heavy auto and foot traffic on Hawthorne Boulevard. "The most unusual experience happened on my way back here. As I drove along the freeway, a message erupted. I'm not sure whether it was a voice from within or without, but an unmistakable message specifically to me."

"What was the message?" Chuck's interest peaked. He leaned forward on his elbows.

"Get out of business. Better prepare yourself to minister My Word. Tell people what great things I have done in your life."

Wide eyed with curiosity, he leaned back and

smirked. "Did they feed you some bad food for lunch up there? Maybe your stomach growled in protest."

"That's an insensitive remark."

I stood up, flashed an expression of disappointment. My unsaved partner knew that his attempt at humor was rejected.

Sitting at my desk behind closed doors, I scanned through the wall of tinted glass windows on my left. Service customers waited in two lines of cars out to the street. *Business is good,* I smiled in an inaudible verbalized thought. Each deep breath eased the tension I had embraced. Business was at an all-time high. My attention shifted to the pile of auto sales contracts on the desk awaiting my review and approval. Mental images of riches and success tranquilized the moment. My senses and breathing pattern settled back to normal, benefiting from each exhalation. Self control, in obedience to the mind's rally to minimize the first-time experience, gave me space to think about doing my job.

Suddenly . . .

"Get out of business."

My throat dried. I thrust backward in the chair, gasping for air. The voice reverberated with greater intensity this time.

"Better prepare yourself to minister My Word."

The flow from my eyes and nose oozed out of control.

***"Tell people what great things
I have done in your life."***

I loosened my tie, looked around for evidence of the form from whence the voice came. There was none. With a handkerchief, I cleared my eyes and nose in suspenseful alert.

Some two years after I committed my life to service in the ministry of Jesus Christ, I had prayed a specific petition to God. By that time I knew Him to be Creator and my heavenly Father. Jesus was my Lord and exclusive access to God. I asked God, in the Name of Jesus, to accept my will, to be used in service of the development of His kingdom here on earth. In my office that day I was positive that after six years He had broken His silence. He spoke to me that day – twice!

Now, after eight years of going to church and Bible study regularly, I was confronted with what I had mistrusted in the confessions of others. People who proclaimed, "God said to me . . ." were on my list of those who I thought sought attention and a reputation of spiritual superiority.

I called Anne. Her voice always calmed me. "Hi, sweetheart. What's happening on the home front?"

"The usual day," she responded. "Never too busy for you though."

"There's something I want to discuss, but in person. What's your schedule look like for the rest of the day?"

"Just picking up Malaika. Is there anything you'd like to talk about now, or can it wait until you get home?

"It's the heaviest load that's ever been delivered to me, but I believe it's an answer to my prayers. I'll be home after I clear up my desk. Love you."

"Love you, too. Can't wait to see you."

Because of the unsettled state of my mind, the rush-hour freeway drive home appeared more challenging. I was relieved to exit at Wilshire Boulevard east but traffic progress stalled at the intersection of Wilshire and Westwood. I thought, *This corner is reported to have one of the highest volumes of cars in our country.* That day was no exception. Many years had passed since Westwood Boulevard was the main artery for my daily trek to the UCLA campus. I looked north toward the entrance but couldn't see past the three blocks of structures. The trance was interrupted by the honk of an impatient soul trying to get out of the gridlock. My heart throbbed. My mind swirled. *What great things was the Voice talking about?*

Four more traffic lights east, I turned left past Westwood United Methodist Church on the northeast corner, worship home of Anne's family during her youth. Three short blocks and I stopped to look at children having fun on the Warner Avenue Elementary School playground. Three of our children were graduated there. Parents in our area confessed openly, It's the best public grammar school in the country.

I turned right onto our street, Loring Avenue. A Presence to alert my eyes to be more aware that I was truly blessed invaded my conscious thought. It amplified the Liquid Amber trees in full fall earth-tone colors lining both sides of the street. They were professionally manicured to accentuate the Kentucky Bluegrass lawns and large multi-storied homes built with a variety of individual architectural expressions which made our street exceptional. The Lord opened my spiritual vision to appreciate that which I had taken for granted.

In the middle of the third block, I pulled into our driveway, sat and pondered the epiphany. I was more convinced now that it was God. I thought, *Socioeconomically, our family life here in this UCLA/Bel Air environment is an abundant example of "what great things God has done in my life." I'm from Watts and this is Westwood,* I said to my soul. I perused our sprawling two-story white stucco, red tile roofed Mediterranean abode. White tile-trimmed walls with black wrought-iron gates surrounded the house and enclosed the front yard and driveway. Our design had drawn rave reviews from neighbors. I mouthed a *Thank you* to God for His immeasurable provisions.

Anne and Malaika greeted me as the car door swung open. "Hi, Daddy. You have a good day at work?"

"Sure did. How was school today?"

Her shrug indicated she didn't hold education in the same esteem as we did. *Not yet*, I reasoned optimistically in thought. "I take that gesture to mean, 'I loved school today, Daddy.'" I picked her hug up and kissed her cheek. "What a beautiful and therapeutic smile. I needed that."

The three of us walked up the front steps, through the arch-covered front porch and oversized dark wood front door. It was as though I entered there for the first time. Everything, by the influence of the Holy Spirit, was exaggerated. The mandate of the epiphany stirred up my consciousness to appreciate that for which I had been less grateful. The large deep reddish brown Spanish tile in the entry and hallway lay regal against the living and dining rooms' plush persimmon carpet. To emphasize the moment, the sun's rays accentuated the pleasing interior design's complement of colors. My senses were filling toward overflowing. Thank you, again, Father God.

The lady who assisted Anne emerged from the kitchen through the hallway separating the breakfast room and dining room. "Hello, Mr. Naulls. I finished my application for citizenship today. Thank you for helping."

"You're welcome, Mima. Anne did all the work – with your help of course. I did pray that your desire would come true before your green card from El Salvador expired. We consider you a member of our family and we love you in the Lord."

"I love all of you too," she smiled.

I thought, *This is like a movie to help me get it. God's at work here right now, and everywhere in my life.*

A half hour passed before we settled. My eyes were on spiritual alert as I continued to scan for evidence of God's blessings. We settled in the sunken living room with its ten-foot ceiling framed by dark wood beams. "Every aspect of this place is my favorite design." Anne agreed. We nestled closer to each other. I admitted to not ever caring for the uncomfortable leather sofa or the matching chairs or the four foot square walnut, beveled glass table. *God, You know my thoughts.* I continued to look around. To the left of the fireplace, through the French doors, I could see the Spanish tiles at water level around the interior of our twenty- by forty-foot swimming pool and Jacuzzi. The herringbone red brick deck and built-in BBQ had fulfilled our family's outdoor leisure dreams. My eyes moistened. *I've been taking so much for granted.* Shannon, our eldest son, stood on the diving board, poised to plunge, as Jonah, our younger son, waited for his turn on the board. Lisa, our Stanford graduate, basked in the sun behind Ray Charles type glasses, reading. Beside us, Malaika finished her piano practice on our seven-foot Steinway as a gentle breeze accompanied her final note of "Für Elise." Yes, these were also examples of the "great things God has done in my life" since my birth in the impoverished and segregated ghetto of Dallas. My eyes overflowed as I turned to Anne.

"What is it, Willie?"

"I heard from God today." Her interest heightened in wide-eyed anticipation of my next words. "On the San Diego Freeway, He said, 'Get out of business. Better prepare yourself to minister My Word. Tell people what great things I have done in your life.'"

A slight smile emerged as her beautiful lips parted to gently speak. "Well, if you know it's God, you'd better do what He says."

There were many responses she could have given that would have encouraged me to stay on the course of my love relationship with business. That would have made it easy to doubt God's call and respond positively to another voice's questions: "Would God really tell you to 'get out of business' when He knows that's your first love? Doesn't He say in His Word to you Christians that He gives you the desires of your hearts?"

"Wherever you go, whatever you determine to

do, I will follow."

My heart warmed as we embraced to seal our covenant with the Lord.

It was settled in my soul and approved by my partner in marriage. We moved "near to God." By doing so, we submitted to His Will to work in and through us to accomplish His good purpose.

God knew the web of our investments and the various stages of development of our business commitments. My prayer, "Lord, you know my comings and goings. You know the thoughts and the intents of my heart. I commit all our cares to You. I know You care for me and my family, for You said if I trust You with all my heart and lean not to my own understanding, but in all my ways acknowledge You, You will direct my path. We rededicate our lives and wills to Your will being done in and through our lives."

Obedience to God's direction produces prosperity in His purpose. My business partner bought total interest in the auto dealership. In three months all of our real estate investments were liquidated. I continued on the path of "better preparing myself to minister His Word" by enrolling in seminary. And over the ensuing years I continue to write down what the Holy Spirit has brought to my mind about "the great things" God has done – and continues to do – in my life.

God demonstrated to me, "If I will trust Him and obey His Word . . . He will . . . ." That Word of Good News applies to every believer who will trust God and obey His Voice.

Count It Pure Joy

I count it pure joy to recall
in the midst of progress and all
God placed a call to my life!
He said, "I've given you much
upward mobility and such
from the depths of poverty – 'I AM' He

. . . .

Oh, I forgot to mention
when the Lord gets your attention
it's a good thing to listen; He'll fill your cup
Know that you have His favor, and just Shut Up!

. . . .

Expanding the Promised Land

The flashing numbers on Anne's cell phone indicated the length of the long distance call. A thought spawned. Our daughter Malaika chose to spend the last semester of study during 2008 in Europe as a University of Texas Law School exchange student. Currently she is in South Africa participating in a program designed by the McCombs Graduate School of Business at UT, visiting selected companies in Johannesburg and Cape Town as well as in Gabarone, Botswana. She appears comfortable traveling 13,000 miles from her place of birth to explore and evaluate international companies as potential partners in business following graduation.

Expanding thoughts of the mental training I was given early in life triggered a widening grin. My heart was energized.

"William, we will not live here in Dallas much longer. Your father and I have decided to move the family to California. Prepare yourself every day for what God is doing. All my Christian life I have longed for us to be free to do and go wherever we chose." She looked upward past the ceiling of our small three-room rented space. "You will live to see a better day. The people in California may not be perfect, but we've heard it's a far better place for you than here. Get ready. My prayers are not unheard. God will change the world so you can go to whatever school you want to study to become your heart's desire – but . . . ." Her eyes shifted from a divine direction to pierce my awaiting psyche. "You have to be prepared. When God opens the door and the world looks beyond its threshold to see what you're made of, you've got to be better prepared, son. Average is not your best effort; neither is good. You have to be at your best or someone else will vault through that door that preparation and opportunity uncover. God's promise to us who love Him is 'I will bless you with the desires of your heart, if you will trust Me and obey My Word.'"

I privately acknowledged her interrupting presence but often did not practice the specifics of her suggestions for any advantage. There were competing screams for my thoughts and decisions.

During the height of attention given author Dr. Bruce Wilkinson's *The Prayer of Jabez* by the international religious community, I reflected again with my life long counselor. She suggested, "Think. Why did God give insight to the author which brought worldwide attention to God's faithfulness to answer prayers?"

I heard a televangelist say, "Jabez was more honorable before God than the other members of the nation Israel. Jabez specifically appealed to God to be 'blessed indeed,' to have his border enlarged and to be kept from evil, that evil would not grieve him."

"Remember our prayers together, William?" Mom's voice resounded clearly, although many years had elapsed since she had expired from her body to eternal life, to rest in the bosom of the Lord's everlasting peace.

Back at my desk, her oration inspired retrospective reflection. God has blessed me indeed. He has answered Mom's prayers. My borders have been enlarged, spiritually, mentally and physically. By conscious choice I desire to grow spiritually through a personal relationship with Jesus Christ; through a pursuit of the understanding of the knowledge of God, I will to make wise decisions. God told Dad and Mom, "Get out of Texas." They heard His command and obeyed. God expanded our family's territorial horizons. He blessed us through expanding our mental and physical development opportunities by moving our family 1,500 miles out of Dallas, into Los Angeles. Communities were integrating. Opportunities to pursue individual excellence and to develop without imposed restrictions of race were liberating. Whom God created me to be was allowed to freely express and to will to compete to be my best, or not. As our geographic borders were enlarged to the shores of the mighty Pacific Ocean, God continued to protect the Naulls family from the evil one. We left grief behind to implode in the souls of satan's territorial agents.

Hindsight can be used effectively as a witness, not only to establish a pattern of results of personal choices to summarize character but, for Christians, to evaluate what great things God has done in response to our prayers. Testimonies of supernatural manifestation in answer to prayers of weeping ordinary people do evidence God honoring His Word. The bottom line of Jabez's prayer: When he called on the God of Israel (the same God my mother called on), "God granted him that which he requested" (I Chronicles 4:10). That is a success model through which all Christians are to be encouraged in our prayer lives. Jabez was a child of God. So are Mom and each member of my family and I. Our prayers were heard. My mom was more honorable before God than most. She bore me in the worst sorrow imaginable, but she was "more honorable before God" than most Christians. God has blessed our family members indeed to the third – now fourth – generation. He expanded our mental and physical horizons to travel around the world as His ambassadors and examples of His faithfulness to bless anyone who trusts Him. He walks with us each step of the way, every day, every night. He gives us renewed strength to trust His Word to stand by faith against grief in victory over the evil one.

As an international ambassador of the USA, I often sensed inner peace traveling, whether in Greenland or Sweden, or looking out the window of a luxurious hotel overlooking the beautiful horseshoe shaped Copa Cabana beach of Rio de Janeiro. Or taking in the view from atop Sugar Loaf Mountain, or peering into the earth's highest lake, Titicaca, in Ecuador. But in each case I knew God was there with me. On the isle of Maui, or on Oahu or the Big Island of Hawai'i to receive the keys to the city of Honolulu or Hilo, or marveling at the engineering feat of the Panama Canal, God was right there with me. Down on the Pacific coast of Antofagasta, Chile, or amid the coup of the Peruvian government in Lima, or communicating with the people of Mexico, Bolivia, Uruguay, Paraguay, Colombia, Argentina, Venezuela, Nicaragua or Costa Rica, or standing in the presence of presidents as an invited guest, God has always been with me wherever I go. How do I know? As a youth, my mother laid her hand on my head and prayed, "Heavenly Father, You are in heaven but you created this world and everything in it. And You honor Your Word to us down here. You promised to walk with us always, Lord, and to talk with us, and You call us Your own. In the Name of Jesus, I thank You in advance for always providing for, protecting and directing our family and for giving us freedom to do our hearts' desires. Deliver us, Lord, from evil men who don't wish us well."

Lisa, our first child, and her son Jonathan represent the third and fourth generation of Naullses who are covered under the wings of the Lord's blessings in answer to Mom's prayers. As was granted to Jabez, her horizons have been extended beyond the scope of her parents and grandparents. A graduate of Stanford University in English Literature and of UCLA's Graduate School of Music, she sings praises to God in opera houses throughout Europe, South America and Asia, as well as in Carnegie Hall and many other venues in America. Her sister Malaika's call from South Africa rekindled in me, as fire shut up in my bones, a zeal to praise the Lord, for He is worthy to be praised for the great things He has done to the third, now fourth generation of Naullses. Praise the Lord! Praise His holy Name!

The Naulls Family

Christmas 1979

Willie • Jonah • Lisa • Shannon • Malaika • Anne

BEWARE

The Christian's Beginning warned
Believers better Beware
The devil's out to entangle
one foot at a time to snare
Temptation lurks around us
Don't allow his leaven to stay
When mixed in the details
evil is headed your way

Perseverance Through Love

God's Word proclaims that from the beginning of creation He has wanted His people to be happy and prosperous. He made everything and declared it to be good. Then He gave this abundantly supplied earth to Adam's dominion. God's plan from the beginning was for man's life to be enriched. Jesus Christ declared that He had come to earth that believers in Him might be redeemed back to God and to dominion in the abundant and eternal life Adam's disobedience had severed .

In the Spirit of fully persuaded faith that God's Word is truth, Anne and I took a leisurely walk near our home. Late May in Spring, Texas, boldly displays brilliant mid-day sunrays peeking from behind puffs of bleached white clouds launched from deep within the heart of the Lone Star State's Big Blue skies. Interrupted occasionally by thundershowers, springtime brings anticipation of outdoor barbeques to celebrate the Spirit of Memorial Day.

About halfway up the driveway of Augusta Pines Golf Course, I slowed to a stop.

"Sometimes I experience uncomfortable pressure in my chest if we walk within two hours of eating."

"Where is the pressure? Is there a sharp pain?"

"No, Anne, there's no pain, just subtle pressure. I've had similar experiences for several years. I'm fine!"

Her brow suggested both intellectual and spiritual concern. "I've already scheduled an appointment for a stress echo-cardiogram the day after we get to California."

"In the good old days of sports, a tightening in the chest was an alarm to 'Suck it up! . . . When the going gets tough, the tough get going . . . No pain – no gain.' . . . Gr-r-r-r!"

"Willie, you and I are both spectators now, so let's get you checked out and know for sure you're as healthy as you proclaim and look. OK?"

There was a seriousness in her voice which I always honor. "God sent you to be my wife and personal physician. I don't believe my health should be of great concern because my last lab numbers, according to Dr. O'Connor, were those of a healthy thirty year old. Can't we trust an endocrinologist's evaluation of my health to include my heart's condition?"

"Not necessarily. That's the reason there are other specialists. We need a cardiologist to check it out."

* * *

Much needed mid-day rain cautioned the drive on the first leg of our mission trip to California. We drove northwest toward Austin on Sunday, 24 May 2009. During a pleasant overnight with our daughter Malaika, we thanked God for the upcoming final year of her University of Texas law and business school trek. She beamed and shared her experiences as a law school exchange student in Milan, Italy, last fall and as part of a graduate business school class in South Africa this spring. After breakfast Monday morning we left for California, staying overnight in Las Cruces, New Mexico, on the way to our destination in Mission Viejo the next afternoon. Lisa and Jonathan welcomed us with open arms into their home.

"Hello, Grandpa! I've been looking for you!"

"My, my, my, Jonathan. You're getting to be a big boy for a three year old. We can spend more time together this trip, if you'd like."

"That's great, Grandpa!" His soft cheek against

mine and tight grip around my neck before he ran off to bed were a blessing to my soul.

"Lisa, I have a doctor's appointment for eight thirty tomorrow morning. Anne has determined, and I concur, that a stress test by a cardiologist is a wise inclusion in my overall annual preventive health plan."

"I agree." Lisa smiled. "Jonathan and I will be praying for you. Good night. Have a pleasant sleep. You guys must be tired. Over 1,500 miles in two days! That's impressive."

Anne spoke up. "We love to drive, and our country is so beautiful."

Dr. Christine Theard of Laguna Niguel, a lean, six-foot Texan with a Jane/Henry Fonda forehead and eye-glare, boldly summarized her examination. "I believe you have a serious blockage in one or more of your heart's arteries. If you don't get it checked out soon, you could drop dead at any time of a heart attack."

I had to respect her efficient use of words. "Anne, how can this be? There's never been any indication of a heart problem during my quarterly checkups."

They both glared toward me and uttered, almost in unison, "An angiogram will disclose the true status of your heart and arteries." Patiently they awaited my decision.

"Well, I trust Anne's empathic concern and I honor your wisdom as a specialist. So, I'm ready for the procedure. What do I do and how long does it take?"

"I used to perform angiograms in the hospital regularly. However, I limited practice to my office after our three-year-old triplets were born. A colleague, Dr. Daniel LaMont, is a specialist in this procedure. If it's all right with you, I'll call and check out his schedule. He's very busy, but the best."

"OK. Thank you." Dr. Theard left us alone in the waiting room of French provincial decor.

"I think you made a wise decision, Willie. Now we will find out for sure why you experience pressure in your chest."

Dr. Theard soon burst back into our presence flashing a gleeful smile. "Good news. Dr. LaMont can see you tomorrow morning at six thirty."

"That's OK with me." My thoughts drifted . . . *What's the rush? Can't they give a guy a few days to . . . what? Why wait?*

"He'll meet you at the hospital – Saddleback Memorial."

Anne and I thanked the good doctor and departed. As we descended in the elevator, she said, "You've made a good decision. You're a man of truth. One of your favorite quotes from the Bible is 'The truth will set you free.' You are a disciple indeed, aren't you?"

We laughed out loud. "You got me this time!"

* * *

We finished all the paperwork by 6:15 a.m., before Dr. LaMont entered. With Hollywood looks and a self-assured USC young professional's confidence, he counseled, "It won't take long, and the procedure is painless." Then it got serious. He and his assistants separated me from my security blanket.

"Mrs. Naulls, will you please go to the waiting room."

"I'll be just down the hall. I love you." Anne disappeared behind swinging doors. I was on my own.

A beautiful young nurse asked, "Mr. Naulls, will you please disrobe entirely?"

She provided a sleeveless pinafore-type garment,

to be held in place by a string tied in a bow at the nape of my neck. It was designed to have a full-length split on my backside and to exaggerate the length of legs supporting my 6′7″ frame.

"Lie on your back on that gurney."

"Yes, ma'am." Very self-conscious, I followed her orders as I reached to pull my "dress" down. The mid-thigh exposure raised thoughts of paranoia about indecent exposure.

Lord, I thought, *You know my heart. You know it's my first experience in this type of situation. I receive Your peace to experience the professionals You have chosen to examine, evaluate, repair and sustain my body until Your created purpose and intent for healing and health takes over. In Jesus' Name, Amen.*

I awoke to Anne's smile. Her face was calming to my spirit and soul. I thought through recovery blinks, *I've just seen Jesus.* A tear of joy threatened to flow.

"How are you feeling?"

"No pain. Have I missed anything?"

"The doctor showed me the video and wants to share the results with you. Dr. LaMont?"

"Willie, you have blockages in all of the major coronary arteries feeding your heart muscle – 100% in two and 80 to 90% in a third. I'm surprised you're still walking around! The good news is your heart is in good shape and functioning normally. Your body has adjusted over the years, producing other vessels for the blood to flow through to feed your heart. I recommend that you have surgery right away to correct this grave situation. You can either be admitted now or come back next week."

I could see Anne's face glowing like an angel from heaven perched beyond my bare size-15 feet, next to yet another "white coat" messenger of truth. "He's staying right here. Let's get this done immediately."

"OK! I have the strength for all things, in Christ, who is my strength."

Dr. LaMont spoke up in earnest report. "Dr. David Perkowski is the best heart surgeon in the world. He's a pioneer in the area of 'off-pump' or 'beating-heart' coronary artery bypass graft surgery and has completed more of those procedures than any other cardiac surgeon. He is also active in clinical research and is widely published on this subject. By the way, he will also appreciate your status as a former professional athlete, as he was an accomplished Olympic swimmer! He understands the importance of bioenergetics in both heart and muscle health. He has 'opened up' a space especially for you tomorrow afternoon at 12:30." A broad grin implied that he enjoyed the humor more than I. "Dr. Perkowski will be here in a little while to meet you."

"Dr. LaMont, I thank God for giving me special favor with you, Dr. Theard and Dr. Perkowski."

* * *

"No one is to be informed of my condition or our decision." I spoke from a lifelong commitment to privacy.

After many words, Anne finally convinced me that "surely our children should be told."

I agreed reluctantly. "No one else, please. Many of our friends and the dear people we know in ministry have serious personal and economic challenges of late and don't need the added weight of Pastor Willie's impending surgery. Promise me, Anne. Don't burden the saints with this news. I'll share God's faithfulness to heal after I'm up on my feet." I looked into her concerned eyes. "Promise me? This is between me and the Lord."

"All right, Willie, but you must call the children

and let them know."

"OK, Sweetheart, and I make you this promise. In one month, in the 29 June 2009 edition of our email newsletter, I will use my health story to share God's faithfulness to His promise to heal His people. I am confident that each of the people we are blessed to serve have prayed for God's work entrusted to us. I believe prayers are stored up in agreement with the Lord's Word: 'According to my faith, be it unto me.' So, in advance, I thank those who have prayed for us in obedience to God's commandment and in response to our appeal in each *Light Bearers Word*."

Anne left around midnight. I was alone in the hospital room with my thoughts, but not for long.

A woman, speaking in broken English, entered. "You William Naulls?"

"Yes, ma'am, I am he."

"I have come to shave your body for operation tomorrow."

Taken by surprise, I replied, "Where is the doctor? Where's my wife? She is a doctor, you know. No one told me that a woman would be shaving me. What part of my body?"

She smirked. "Your whole body," gesturing up and down with her pointing finger.

"I'll call my wife."

At that moment, a doctor I had not met before appeared with assistants. "I'm an associate of Dr. Perkowski. We're here to go over what the operation intends to accomplish." At the end of his very informative lecture, he said, with a smile from ear to ear, "The body barber is legitimate. Cleansing of hair from your body is necessary prior to the operation."

"OK, doc, I understand."

A little later . . . "I take your gown off now, OK?" She mounted the side of the bed with a razor in hand and proceeded to rid my nude body of hair. I closed my eyes and wondered whether this was a barbaric world in which my wife and her peers had left me to survive.

My mind shifted to the line of the song, *"What a Friend We Have in Jesus."* The choir in heaven led: *"Oh, what peace we often forfeit. Oh, what needless cares we bear. Just because we do not carry everything to God in prayer."*

* * *

The next morning I was able to spend some time with Anne, Lisa, our older son Shannon and his wife, Tammy. We talked and they read some of our favorite Scriptures from the Bible. The UCLA-trained anesthesiologist came in and explained his part in the procedure. After listening intently, my family prayed and kissed me as I was being wheeled into the operating room.

"We love you, Dad."

"I love you, babe. I love you all too and I'll see you soon" accompanied my wave of faith.

It was like a Hollywood drama, but I was the star in this real life event. My mind started on a "what if" trip. As I looked into the eyes of the anesthesiologist, he asked, "How are you doing, Willie? You ready?"

A calm flushed my mind and body. My eyes dimmed. A slight quiver of lips as my heart whispered, "It is written . . . ."

* * *

The next conscious memory: awakening in the recovery room after three-plus hours of corrective surgery of my body's most essential system.

"Welcome back, Pastor Willie. The procedure went fabulously well. Dr. Perkowski is the best." The nurse's eyes beamed a smile which caught hold of my inner man.

"Praise the Lord!"

"Amen and amen," she responded.

My speech was affected by what the nurse identified as pain killers. I did not feel pain but soon became aware of the evidence of what had been done to my body to accomplish the mission of the surgery. There were tubes and drain lines affixed to my chest and neck. Their purpose was to monitor my bodily functions and facilitate the elimination of waste associated with the healing process God created in our bodies.

After two days in the intensive care unit, I was transferred to a semi-private room. People from every department who served Dr. LaMont's and Dr. Perkowski's patients came to visit. God was glorified for His faithfulness, mercy and loving kindness through the people He chose to serve my needs.

I was released after five days. With the use of a walker, I settled into the passenger seat of our car. "Hallelujah! Anne. I'm on the way to full recovery!" I paused to kiss her and thank her for being so obvious about her love for me.

"It's good to be alive. God has healed me to continue to tell people what great things He has done, is doing, and will continue to do in the lives of people who diligently pursue Him. What a great experience to meet so many wonderful people. Wow! Thank God. I praise Him for He alone is worthy to be praised."

* * *

A few days later, internist Dr. Gabrielle O'Connor, my prime-time and esteemed physician, gave me her sage advice: "An almost forgotten word in the English language is one I suggest you embrace: Convalescence. Don't rush or be anxious or discouraged. You are ahead of the normal recovery time, in your mind. Follow the advice of your doctors. Listen to the Spirit's direction to your body and you'll be in God's timing."

After final visits with four other doctors, Dr. O'Connor gave me the fifth OK to drive back to Texas. "We agreed – doctors Chang, Theard, LaMont, Perkowski and I – that the final decision on when you're well enough to drive rests solely in the discretion of Anne. We all suggest that you research to find a good cardiologist and cardiac rehabilitation center to monitor your progress over the next year. Your body is just beginning to recover. You must practice living a quality lifestyle to allow the maximum potential of recovery of all of your systems." She smiled. "Just do what your wife tells you!"

Gabrielle and Anne glowed a knowing, confident stand in righteousness that only the truth reveals.

* * *

We departed Mission Viejo around noon the next day. Another beautiful trip, with overnight stays in Las Cruces and with Malaika in Austin. The first big post-operative challenge was climbing the 40 stairs up to her condo. She and Anne left me with Cleo the cat to rest in a comfortable, oversized black leather chair while they did whatever it is they enjoy so much whenever they're together. My mind settled in the bosom of the Lord. A song ministered by Lisa, graciously dedicated to Anne and me during church services the previous Sunday, overwhelmed my heart in praise and thanksgiving to God. My mind filled to overflowing. The angelic choir began to hum in my soul "More Than Wonderful."

He promised us that He would be a Counselor
A Mighty God and the Prince of Peace
He promised us that He would be a Father
And that He would love us with a love that
would not cease . . . .

Our Lord is **more than wonderful**! Today, 29 June 2009, is exactly one month removed from that day when God used His professionals to confirm the length and quality of the abundant life He promised me in His Son.

Friendship sent by the Lord is like mining for gold, rare to unearth, rare to unfold!

Bill Withers & Willie Naulls

Bill called a Friends' Summit atop the cliffs of the Pacific Ocean at the Montage Resort in Laguna Beach to offer compassion to "Lean On [Him]" one month after Willie's quadruple bypass surgery.

Anne and I were privileged to be invited special guests as Stanford University Medical School honored life-long friend
Augustus A. White, III, M.D., Ph.D
with its Lifetime Achievement Award.
Gus was the first African-American gradate of the Medical School and the first African-American surgical resident at Yale-New Haven Hospital. He is currently Professor of Orthopaedics Emeritus at Harvard School of Medicine.

Anita • Gus • Willie • Anne

So . . . Friendship is like Love to behold,
without spot or wrinkle, when valued as gold.

About Willie Naulls

"Get out of business and better prepare yourself to minister My Word and tell people what great things I have done in your life."

When Willie Naulls heard God speak these words to him in 1991, he obeyed. Because of his diligence in seeking to learn all he could about the Christianity to which he had committed his life, he had already undertaken three years of study at the Ministry Training Institute in Los Angeles. He had also begun coursework toward a Master's Degree in Theology at Fuller Theological Seminary while continuing his various business pursuits. This full-time call to ministry prompted him to sell all of his businesses in order to spend full time on his studies.

In 1993, Willie founded Willie Naulls Ministries. He converted a 63,000 square foot aerospace building on a 5.75 acre leased property into a multi-purpose facility. The development included a sanctuary, offices, restaurant, training rooms and athletic courts for basketball and volleyball. In this space, he pursued his passion for inspiring young people, encouraging them to work out of themselves the industry God had put into each individually. Willie has concentrated his time on mentoring individuals and speaking to youth and men's groups since the end of the lease on that facility. In addition, he has completed the books outlined below as well as a training manual on cultural sensitivity. He continues to pursue his dream of building a facility to house all of the ministry works God has put in his heart.

The mission of Willie Naulls Ministries is to equip believers to shine like stars in the universe as they live out the Word of Life (Philippians 2:12-16a). His outreach to junior and senior high school students and their parents is founded on Christian principles. The thrust of God's work is specifically designed to maximize the development of their God given talents through academic, athletic and spiritual leadership training and development. The desired result is maturing these students to live in God's purpose for their lives as they prosper to serve others.

Pastor, husband, father of four, and grandfather of four, Willie Naulls is the author of several books and motivational pamphlets, including two volumes of his memoirs, ***Levitation's View: Lessons Voiced from an Extraordinary Journey.***

The work of Willie Naulls Ministries is supported by the free-will offerings of our partners and vision supporters and by contributions from readers inspired by the message of Willie's books.

We encourage you to visit our website: *www.willienaulls.org*. Sign up to receive the "Light Bearers Word" email newsletter. Encourage your church and organizations to invite Willie to speak and share his vast wealth of knowledge and experience. Pray that the Lord will continue to bless His work at Willie Naulls Ministries so that many will be encouraged to work out of themselves what God has placed in them, to His glory.

The William D. Naulls Family

1991

Anne • Malaika • Lisa
Jonah • Willie • Shannon

About Lisa Naulls

Lisa Naulls is a professional vocalist and private vocal coach to both adults and youth. She has been a featured soloist in such venues as the Hollywood Bowl and Carnegie Hall in the United States as well as concert halls throughout Europe, Asia and South America. She has sung with numerous philharmonic orchestras including those in Berlin, Vienna and Hawaii. Lisa has performed and lectured to youth as part of the Guild Opera Education Outreach program. She is the Director of BASIC, an *a cappella* vocal quartet featuring music for the holidays and other special events. Lisa has developed an educational program for youth in which she teaches children as young as five to sing in seven languages. The sessions introduce the children to the fundamentals of music, voice, movement, story development and stage production. Classes culminate in a musical production including the spoken word, dance/movement, and vocals with live and/or prerecorded music.

A graduate of Stanford University in English Literature, Lisa earned a Master's Degree in Vocal Performance from the Graduate School of Music at UCLA.

Following a recent solo concert, she received an email from a woman in the audience:

"Dear Lisa,

"I want to thank you from the bottom of my heart for that spectacular performance on Saturday night. Not only did you create an environment that allowed us to partake in the beautiful holiday music; you brought a sense of joy and optimism for the coming year in a way that a sermon and prayers said by rote simply cannot do. The duet of Avinu Malkeinu ("Our Father, Our King") ranks among the most magnificent I have ever heard, and I was humming it all day on Sunday. Thank you for bringing such joy and harmony to our group."

Willie & Lisa, at age four

I've had the opportunity over the course of my life to express how God has blessed me – through song, education, career, family. Now I have been presented with a new medium of expression ... the published word!

My beloved dad has invited me to join with him in the auspicious ranks of published author. His new book featuring shared stories of triumph over disease, daily trials, love challenges – in essence, "the stuff of life" – will illustrate beyond doubt that God, through it all, is God. The same, yesterday, today, and forever. And He's STILL in the blessing business.

I'm excited and humbled to now be a part of my father's impressive book collection. All of his books are insightful, Spirit-filled, and accessible. They teach, soothe, amuse, and challenge. Anyone curious about race relations at the crest of integrated sports, the secret to professional athletic success alongside the likes of Bill Russell and Wilt Chamberlain, and balancing fame with family will be entertained and edified.

I'm truly blessed to be a part of this book.

Lisa Naulls

Other Books by Willie Naulls

Levitation's View: Lessons Voiced from an Extraordinary Journey: Volume I: The Wonder Years begins with Willie's early years in a ghetto of Dallas, Texas, where he was born. At nine years of age, he moved with his family to predominantly White San Pedro, the harbor community of Los Angeles, California. There he developed into an All-City athlete in two sports. The book is the recollection of a Black skinned child facing a difficult world, both surviving and thriving because of the Christian values taught and lived before him by his mother.

Levitation's View: Volume II: The Wooden Years tells the story of the relationship between two UCLA Hall of Famers: a maturing All-American basketball player, and a developing all-time winning coach, John Wooden. It is a provocative account of the life lessons learned by an introspective and pioneering athlete as he moved from the ghetto of Watts into the upper class community of Westwood Village and UCLA. Together he and Coach Wooden surfed the wave of integration of NCAA Basketball.

A Guide to Building Character in Blocks of Poetic Rhyme draws from Willie's many years of Biblical study and teaching experience to define salient qualities of a person of Godly character. Photo images in the book honor selected individuals of demonstrated high character who are role models for our youth. The messages of the building blocks teach the importance of living by the high standards of the Word of God.

Black – On Up Off Of My Back: Poems from a Voice swept under the carpet of the Black Skin enigma Willie's book of poetry will inspire anyone who has been burdened by negative stereotypes of genetic or cultural origin. The intent of this poetic expression is to engage thought processes and to influence change in the way we look at people of different races.

Book Request Form
on reverse side

Request for Books

The work of Willie Naulls Ministries is supported by donations from our partners and vision supporters and by contributions from readers inspired by the message of Willie's books.

The suggested donation for each book is $25.00. Thank you for your support!

For bulk orders, please e-mail: anne@willienaulls.org

Please ship the following order to:

Name:____

Address:______________________________________

City, State, ZIP:________________________________

E-mail Address:________________________________

Please send me your email newsletters! _____

	Number	Donation
***Levitation's View, Volume I: The Wonder Years*....... **	_______	$_______
***Levitation's View, Volume II: The Wooden Years*.... **	_______	$_______
***A Guide to Building Character in Blocks of Poetic Rhyme*.................................**	_______	$_______
***Black – On Up Off Of My Back*....................................**	_______	$_______
***Great Things God Has Done* ....**	_______	$_______
My tax deductible gift to Willie Naulls Ministries....................		$_______
Total enclosed (check or money order please)............		$_______

Please send your check payable to Willie Naulls Ministries to:

Willie Naulls Ministries
Post Office Box 132888
Spring, Texas 77393-2888